R U #SoLoMo Ready?

R U #SoLoMo Ready?

Consumers and Brands in the Digital Era

Dr. Stavros Papakonstantinidis,
Dr. Athanasios Poulis and
Dr. Prokopis Theodoridis

BEP BUSINESS EXPERT PRESS

R U #SoLoMo Ready? Consumers and Brands in the Digital Era

Copyright © Business Expert Press, LLC, 2016

First published in 2016 by
Business Expert Press, LLC
222 East 46th Street, New York, NY 10017
www.businessexpertpress.com

ISBN-13: 978-1-63157-256-2 (paperback)
ISBN-13: 978-1-63157-257-9 (e-book)

Business Expert Press Digital and Social Media Marketing and Advertising Collection

Collection ISSN: 2333-8822 (print)
Collection ISSN: 2333-8830 (electronic)

Cover and interior design by S4Carlisle Publishing Services Private Ltd., Chennai, India

First edition: 2016

10 9 8 7 6 5 4 3 2 1

Printed in the United States of America.

Abstract

In today's highly cluttered digital marketing environment there is a great need for marketers to fully comprehend a new breed of consumers. This book introduces the rising trend of SoLoMo consumers who embrace an omnichannel marketing approach. Nowadays, consumers are rapidly moving between channels and platforms, and that is why marketers are finding it so difficult to implement an integrated marketing strategy. Today's consumers can check into a store with the use of a geolocation service (Foursquare), redeem an offer that is available, and share their comment on that platform. Then immediately they can post an update on their Facebook timeline, referencing the retailer's page. SoLoMo consumers have three basic characteristics: SOcial media engagement, LOcal findability, and smartphone MObility. In the following chapters, the authors conceptualize this new marketing approach, while providing examples to illustrate the case. The SoLoMo phenomenon has completely changed the way marketers have to operate their campaigns, from the way they even conceive of their relationship with the customer through to the way they design and operate campaigns themselves. The crux of the matter is that there has been a convergence in marketing as much as there has been a convergence in technology.

Keywords

SoLoMo consumer, digital marketing, mobile marketing, social media, social entertainment, geolocation

Contents

Preface

This book aims to explore the SoLoMo experience in digital marketing. SoLoMo is a marketing approach in which Social, Local, and Mobile converge. Back in the 1960s, marketers' job was quite straightforward. All they had to do was to come up with an informative, catchy advertisement and place it on the media (TV, radio, press, outdoor). Mom and dad would watch the advertisement to decide whether they needed to buy this product or not. Many years later, in the 1990s, marketers were already the experts in launching campaigns, conceptualizing the importance of the strong message that builds brands. People loved the branding.

Today, things are not straightforward. Modern marketers who simply launch campaigns with catchy advertising messages will eventually fail. Why? There are two reasons. The first reason is brands are different. They are not based on a catchy message telling people to do this or the other. Modern brands offer a digital experience inviting consumers to join. They shape people's realities and offer solutions to real-life situations. As soon as the brand develops a new experience both digital and traditional marketing tools invite consumers to join.

This new digital experience demands the development of new strategies that bring closer social, mobile, and local marketing. In other words, today's marketers are like good hosts of a big party with many guests. Not only they have to organize the party, they need to make sure the party will be successful and no guest will leave complaining. Brand reputation matters more than brand recall.

The second reason is consumers are different too. Modern consumers are elusive, tech-savvy, content-oriented, omnichannel shoppers, collaborators, and social sharers (Bolen, 2015). Trendwatching (2014) calls them presumers, producers, and consumers at the same time. Presumers are willing to buy a product or enjoy a service and then write about their experience on their personal social networks. Modern consumers are digital storytellers like marketers. With the rapid proliferation of social media and mobile devices, consumers have strengthened their position as valid opinion leaders. Who is stronger anymore? A newspaper that sells 1,000 issues a day or a Twitter user with millions of followers?

Imagine a young college student, back in 1995, who is working part-time for an electronics retail store. He takes his job seriously and gives his best to serve every customer. In our hypothetical story, his high quality of customer service is appreciated by a gentleman who kindly sends a letter to the young salesman's supervisor, thanking him and the company for their dedication to excellence.

Today, the same customer would have done things differently. As we are all witnessing the age of digital consumers, our story's customer would post his positive opinion on the company's Facebook page, tweet with a relevant hashtag to his Twitter followers, give thumbs up on the product's YouTube channel, mention his new gadget on Instagram, write on his blog, leave a review on Yelp or Google Reviews, and so on.

What has actually changed over the last 20 years? The rapid proliferation of the web and more specifically of social media have changed how people communicate, stay informed, get entertained, and do business (Qualman, 2009). Nowadays, the new consumer feels more important than the brand. He understands that his voice is enough to have an impact on other people's decision-making process.

The new consumer is able to produce content anywhere, at any moment, and to anyone. Nothing is private anymore. Reviews, either positive or negative, are to be shared. Social networking sites are the modern megaphones of messages while consumers are using them to share their stories in far-reaching and widely public and digital avenues.

The new consumers do not simply consume or love brands. They breathe them. They produce their own content by posting or commenting on others' posts. In addition, modern consumers are addicted to their mobile devices, checking on their smartphones, tablets, or both for almost three hours each day (Brustein, 2014). For the first time in the history of media, in 2014, people spent more time on their mobile devices than TV (Flurry Analytics, 2015).

As consumers are rapidly moving between channels and platforms, marketers are finding it so difficult to implement an integrated marketing strategy. In today's highly cluttered digital marketing environment there is a great need for marketers to fully comprehend a new breed of consumers. For example, the modern consumer can check into a store with the use of a geolocation service (i.e., Foursquare, Google+, Facebook check-in), redeem an offer that is available only for those consumers who are online, pay with Android Pay or Apple Pay, and share his or her comments on social media.

Apparently the new consumer is not simply digitalized. The new consumer is SoLoMo. This book introduces the rising trend of SoLoMo consumers who have three basic characteristics: **SO**cial media engagement, **LO**cal findability, and phone **MO**bility. SoLoMo stands for Social, Local, and Mobile, combining the best of all aspects of digital and traditional marketing. Smartphones are empowering consumers and transforming shopping and recreational behaviors. Shopping used to be fun. Now it is much more than that. It is a game with immediate rewards and a chance to get in touch with friends and followers. Inevitably, marketing is becoming Phygital—physical and digital work together, simultaneously and interdependently.

Through this book we aim to explore the impact of Social, Local, and Mobile characteristics on digital marketing. Why SoLoMo? SoLoMo describes the environment in which consumers share their experiences online, form digital communities, trust their peers' reviews more than the brand's, search for nearby stores (retails, restaurants, bars, etc.), and check in at their favorite local businesses.

In the following chapters, we will conceptualize this new mindset, while providing examples to illustrate the case. The target audiences of the book are marketing practitioners, digital marketing consultants, entrepreneurs, PR executives, and students of marketing and digital communications. The next section provides a brief description of each chapter to show a logical structure from the introduction to conclusions and future implications.

Setting the Scene

Chapter One introduces the reader to the SoLoMo experience in digital marketing. Primarily, however, it briefly defines essential tools of digital marketing to help the reader shape a clearer view of the digital marketing landscape. Then, we signify the SoLoMo concept's importance in marketing literature by mainly explaining its impact on consumers and brands. As users are being transformed into presumers, producers, and consumers at the same time (Trendwatching, 2014), the web becomes a more semantic environment, with its own culture and set of expected consumer behaviors. Therefore, the first chapter presents the general characteristics of the new, more digital-oriented user, the SoLoMo consumer.

In **Chapter Two** the SoLoMo consumer goes social. In today's turbulent environment the "new" types of consumers no longer look to brands as the primary source of information. SoLoMo consumers are more likely to consult a third-party resource and others in the social networks they are engaging to. Some common social activities that they are performing are seeking advice, reading or writing reviews, or sharing experiences via a social network. In this chapter the authors are going to extensively analyze the following topics:

- SoLoMo consumers are social
- New trends in social engagement (social search, visual search, content marketing, social commerce)
- Twitter, Facebook, and Instagram as entry points to purchase
- The YouTube community and social entertainment (product reviews, home videos, song covers, thumbs up, dislikes)
- Use of collective coupons (Groupon)
- Seek recommendations through social networks
- Case analysis

In **Chapter Three** the SoLoMo consumer searches locally. Consumers are submitting more and more location data, with the use of geolocation techniques. Social networks, such as Foursquare and Google Places, use these data of information in order to connect and coordinate users with local people or events that match their interests in the highest possible degree. In this chapter the authors are going to extensively analyze the following topics:

- SoLoMo consumers are local
- Characteristics of their local behavior
- Geosocial networking
- New trends in geolocation services
- Use of geosocial applications (such as Foursquare) to check in
- NFC payments
- Use of coupons
- Use of beacons
- Benefits of geolocation services

Chapter Four presents the mobile characteristic of the SoLoMo consumer. It is estimated that over 4.55 billion people worldwide use a mobile phone in 2014 (Pew Research, 2015). In addition, the global smartphone audience surpassed the 1 billion mark in 2012 and will total 1.75 billion in 2014. SoLoMo consumers rely heavily on their smartphones spending an enormous amount of time checking for messages, social updates, and online information. In this chapter the authors are going to extensively analyze the following topics:

- SoLoMo consumers are mobile
- Characteristics of consumers' mobile behavior
- New trends in mobile marketing
- Multiscreen behavior
- Mobile marketing strategy

The last three chapters suggest strategies for brands to apply the SoLoMo strategy to today's marketing. **Chapter Five** discusses a variety of digital marketing and SoLoMo-oriented strategies to provide the readers with full understanding of how SoLoMo marketing can be applied. It also discusses several SoLoMo applications to provide the reader with the necessary digital, social, local, and mobile tools to apply the I.N.T.E.R.A.C.T. model to their marketing strategies. More specifically, this chapter discusses the following:

- The mobile web
- Digital marketing tools
- Social tools
- Local tools
- Mobile tools
- The I.N.T.E.R.A.C.T. model
- Implications for marketers

Chapter Six concludes with a forecast on digital marketing's next day. How is the SoLoMo consumer able to shape the current online environment? What brands should do to embrace the new breed of consumers? This chapter examines how new technologies will affect and be embraced by the SoLoMo consumer, such as NFC payment and wearable items. Whether we are right or wrong in our predictions nobody knows. The future will tell...

CHAPTER 1

The Rise of SoLoMo

In this chapter you will read:

- About the new marketing landscape
- Facts about social media
- Facebook facts
- Twitter facts
- LinkedIn facts
- Google+ facts
- Instagram facts
- Pinterest facts
- Other facts
- Social media's impact on society
- About the SoLoMo consumer

Introduction

Nobody can predict the future. But as consumers change, marketing has to change too. Its role in the evolution of business is essential to identify and address the modern consumer behaviors. As a well-developed scientific field, marketing is constantly adapting its methods and strategies to fully meet the new consumer needs.

In *Winning the Zero Moment of Truth*, Jim Lecinski (2012, p.11) writes about the customer's multiplatform journey that *the shopper's journey looks less like a funnel and more like a flight map. Shoppers dart back and forth as they touch down—again and again—not at cities but at all the information hubs on their journey.* The new consumer starts his journey from online search engines (Lecinski, 2012). Other sources of influence such as traditional media (TV, Radio, Print, Outdoor, etc.) as well as in-store marketing in brick-and-mortar stores play a supplementary role.

According to Ericsson Mobility Report (2015), around 7.2 billion mobile subscriptions were reported in Q1 2015. Furthermore, 108 million new mobile users were added the first four months of 2015. What is more impressive is the report's prognosis that smartphone subscriptions will be more than double by 2020, which means that 70 percent of the world's population will own at least one smartphone. In addition, Ericsson Mobility Report (2015) forecasts the connected devices (smartphones, tablets, and phablets) will be 26 billion by 2020.

The digital world will be based on mobility as the numbers of mobile applications and mobile data traffic are rapidly increasing. The global digital agency "We are Social" argues in its Digital Statshot Report (Kemp, 2015) that *mobile will help to push internet penetration beyond 50% of the world's population during mid to late 2016.* As connected devices and mobile data become more affordable, people will ubiquitously connect online, through a wide variety of mobile applications like WhatsApp, WeChat, and Facebook Messenger achieving the top ranking spots in social media around the world.

The current and expected growth of connected devices in social networks develops a new marketing environment which will be based on three pillars.

1. Consumers are getting Social.
   Social networking sites like Facebook, Twitter, and Instagram are growing rapidly as channels of human communication allowing brands and consumers to engage in public discussions. As consumers are using social media as their main source of information, communication, and entertainment, marketers will be finding a fruitful environment full of opportunities.
2. Consumers are checking Local.
   The rapid proliferation of advanced smartphone and other mobile devices allowed people to exchange information by pinpointing consumers' location and providing them on their mobile devices with location-specific advertisements. The integration of mobile advertising with location-based services is what characterizes location-based advertising.

3. Consumers are becoming Mobile.

As presented at Internet Trends 2015—Code Conference by Kleiner Perkins Caufield & Byers (KPCB)—mobile digital media time has already overtaken desktop and other media Internet access. Smartphone penetration has increased for two reasons. First, wireless networks have become faster and ubiquitous. Second, mobile devices are nowadays more affordable. Mobile marketing can provide consumers with personalized information based on their location and the time of receipt. To use simple words, consumers are more attached to their phones than their personal computers, providing marketers with new tools and opportunities to *fish where the fish are.*

This leads us to the assumption that the study of the convergence of social media expansion, location-based services, and mobile usage becomes a necessity in digital marketing. As mentioned above, SoLoMo stands out for Social, Local, and Mobile. It is an emerging marketing concept that can make use of modern digital marketing tools.

In today's marketing environment everybody has a voice. Consumers have their own voice. Brands can reply. Social media is not simply used by people. Products and brands have their own accounts as well. For instance, the official match ball of the 2014 World Cup Brazuca was given human characteristics through a creative and anthropomorphic Twitter account. @Brazuca started tweeting seven months prior to the official start of the World Cup 2014. Adidas used Twitter in the most appropriate way to apply SoLoMo marketing, initiating a variety of human discussions with its over 3.4 million followers, including famous brand ambassadors such as David Beckham, Pharrel Williams, and Zinedine Zidane.

Using Brazuca's Twitter hashtag, the #ballin is everywhere and anywhere. It is not anymore about simply selling. It is about establishing connections. Brands want to be like humans, and humans want to be like brands. Consumers are surrounded by a plethora of marketing tools and applications. Search engines, optimized websites, responsive platforms, Facebook pages, digital advertisements, video campaigns, Twitter accounts, Instagram hashtags, etc., are part of the game. Mobile marketing, location-based services, e-mail marketing with opt-in mailing lists, affiliate marketing, online public relations, article syndication, advertorials, referrals, and back links create a new marketing landscape in which the brand needs to have a loud and consistent voice. Otherwise, brands and consumers will never manage to meet. The following section provides a brief overview of the new marketing landscape.

The New Marketing Landscape

Advertising blooms from the early existence of humanity. People have the need to influence other people, using any mean they have. Until recently brands relied heavily on traditional marketing tools such as television ads, print ads, brochures, posters, and radio ads to communicate with their target markets. Now, with the rapid development of the Internet, brands communicate directly with their consumers seeking for immediate and accurate feedback.

The desire of every business or brand is primarily to approach new customers, then progressively to build relationships with them, and finally to convert them to loyal customers and lead them to purchasing. In that purpose, digital marketing has distinct differences from traditional marketing. In digital marketing the achievement of acquisition, conversion, and retention may be fulfilled with different manners (Chaffey and Ellis-Chadwick, 2012). It depends on the product or service that someone wants to promote, the needs, or even the target audience that refers to. There is not an ideal marketing plan in the digital world; there are always different solutions.

We used to say that a marketing plan needs to master the 4Ps: Product, Place, Price, and Promotion. Today, in addition to what traditional marketing dictates, we need to know what the customer thinks and how he or she behaves before, during, and after the purchase. Knowing the variety of different channels that can be used in the new marketing landscape, a consumer can be approached through a well-structured website, social networking sites, blogs, or mobile apps.

In order for a digital marketing campaign to be successful, it is crucial that both the online and offline marketing techniques have to integrate properly. Rolling out a digital marketing campaign can be challenging. Thus, a wise selection of acquisition, conversion, and retention tools is essential (Chaffey and Ellis-Chadwick, 2012) to guide modern consumers to their digital and physical customer journey.

In other words, the acquisition tools are used for starting the customer cycle, focusing on selecting the right target audience and emphasizing on establishing the relationship between the customer and the product. Conversion tools, on the other hand, aim to persuade customers to act by proceeding on the purchase of the product (Chaffey and Ellis-Chadwick, 2012). Finally, after the customer–product relationship has started, the brand's main goal is to keep its existing customers and turn them into loyal, returning customers. In order to do so, retention tools are used, so that the company's products will be always on the radar of the existing customers. To better illustrate the wide variety of available "stops" in customer journey, the following table classifies the acquisition, conversion, and retention tools in digital marketing (Econsultancy, 2014).

Acquisition Tools	Conversion Tools	Retention Tools
Search Engine Optimization	Mapping Your Sales Process	Ask for Options
PPC Advertising	Accessibility	Measure Lifetime Value
Facebook Ads	Customer Support	E-mail Marketing
Social Media Marketing	Personalization and Targeting	Direct E-mail
Online PR	E-mail Marketing	Premium and Gifts
Content Marketing	Onsite Search	FAQ
Special Events and Promotions	Design Optimization	CRM Systems
Link Building	A/B Testing	Questionnaires and Surveys
	Live Help	Community Referrals
	Measure Conversion Rate	Social Media
	Social Media Monitor Tools	Personalization Website
	Keyword Monitor Tools	Loyalty Programs

Today's customer journey is greatly affected by social media, local marketing, and mobile applications. The following section discusses a 2014 study by Pew Research about teens, social media, and technology.

As smartphones and mobile telecommunication companies offer constant and high-speed online access, 92% of teenagers answered that they go online daily, and 24% almost constantly (Pew Research, 2015). Much of teenagers' (aged 13–17) access is facilitated through mobile devices (smartphones, tablets), with Facebook (71%) being the most popular social media platform among them. In addition, according to Pew Research (2015), other than Facebook, the most popular social media platforms for teenagers are Instagram (52%), Snapchat (41%), Twitter (33%), Google+ (33%), Vine (24%), and Tumblr (14%).

It is quite impressive that YouTube is not one of teenagers' options. Nevertheless, 71% of them logs in to more than one social networking sites. The terms social networking sites and Web 2.0 are widely discussed in a range of industries, such as advertising, marketing, web development, and human resources. Both terms, however, are elusive since they are constantly adjusting to new realities that online users shape. Social networks are the

> "activities, practices, and behaviors among communities of people who gather online to share information, knowledge, and opinions using conversational networks. Conversational networks are web-based applications that make it possible to create and easily transmit content in the form of words, pictures, videos and audios" (Safko and Brake, 2009, p.6).

The narrow concept of social networks includes not only the well-versed social networking sites such as Facebook, Twitter, and LinkedIn, but it also consists of blogs (online journals), forums, wikis, and virtual worlds. In a wider definition, the social networks are referred by websites that share common characteristics in the sense of developing online communities that promote communication and self-expression (Santonocito, 2009). Social networks also include the more recent concepts of open-source-generated content, which is too technical to be discussed in this dissertation. Nevertheless, a main characteristic of social networks, although a bit simplistic, is that online users are able to generate content and to promote it through the web by sharing links with the online Web 2.0 communities.

The social networking sites affect the way companies promote their products, communicate with their consumers and employees, and recently organize their recruitment practices. An essential aspect of social networks is the need of online users to participate instead of simply retrieving information. Social networks users are willing to share personal information online. However, as Murugesan (2007) argues, they follow a set of rules and norms that do not violate the community's expectations. This characteristic is what makes online social networks such a powerful communication and business tool.

The main characteristic of a social networking site is the sense of community that the traditional web sites cannot develop. Many examples of social networks prove that today's administrations are gradually using it for their benefit. Social networking sites, blogs, wikis, and forums are low-cost advertising and communication platforms that further engagement with customers and users of the Internet (Miller and Lammas, 2010).

Facts about Social Media

The use of social networks is extremely popular among digital consumers. The numbers are dazzling. According to Kemp (2015), 3.65 billion users access the Web via their mobile devices (smartphones, tablets, laptops, etc.). As per the official data given by Facebook, Twitter, Google+, Linkedin, Instagram, and Pinterest, almost 1.7 billion people have active social media accounts.

It is almost impossible to define something that is constantly changing and adapting to new realities. Boyd and Ellison (2008) make an interesting distinction between the words network and networking. The authors argue that the term networking refers to connections among strangers while people network with those who know. Even if someone might claim that people use the social media to communicate with their friends, reality has shown that the social media allows users to interact with each other regardless their level of familiarity.

In an attempt, though, to explain what social networking sites are, Boyd and Ellison (2008, p. 210) define them as "web-based services that allow individuals to (1) construct a public or a semi-public profile within a bounded system, (2) articulate a list of other users with whom they share a connection, and (3) view and traverse their list of connections and those made by others within the system." The latter authors' definition argues that the system in which online communication takes place has certain boundaries and limitations. In fact, scholars are still not clear as to the pure nature of those sites and their potentialities.

Social networking sites are online platforms designed by users who constantly add new features on the Internet to serve a wide and growing variety of consumer needs (Weaver and Morrison, 2008). It is almost impossible to provide an accurate number as to how many social networking sites are currently operating, or how many people are actually active on social media. Following, this section quotes from Digital Statshot Report (Kemp, 2015) some interesting statistics and facts about the most popular social networking sites.

Facebook facts

Facebook is the most popular social networking site with nearly 1.4 billion users (nearly 47% of all Internet users). Facebook was created in 2003 to primarily connect Harvard University classmates. Then it is expanded to connect friends in different universities in the United States, but soon it became widely known to the overall population. Facebook offers a wide range of features and applications to its users to connect with friends online, find old classmates, join in groups and other networks, post images, videos, hyperlinks, thoughts, and personal updates. The most popular feature is the Like buttons that is hit 4.5 billion times per day.

Twitter facts

Microblogging services are online social networks that allow users to post instantly their thoughts and to share their favorite links. The most popular microblogging social networking site is Twitter with 284 million active users as of December 2014.

Using Twitter, the registered users can send short 140-character messages (tweet) expressing personal thoughts or posting the URL address of interesting articles. There are 500 million tweets per day. Twitter uses the term *follower* to describe those users who are following other Twitter accounts (persons and organizations). The general idea of Twitter is simple and straight forward that makes it very attractive to the online users, with 88% of them to access it through their mobile devices.

LinkedIn facts

LinkedIn is one of the oldest social networking sites, having started in 2002. LinkedIn has 347 million registered members and is considered the professional Facebook. LinkedIn has a more professional nature compared to Facebook's social and friendly nature. Using LinkedIn, the users upload their resumes, make professional connections, and emphasize on their professional and academic credentials. More than 39 million of LinkedIn's users are college students and recent graduates.

Google+ facts

Google+ is Google's social network and according to the same company, "a social layer across all of Google's services." It is the newest of the popular social media, offering almost similar services and features with Facebook and Twitter. Probably this is the main reason why Google's half a billion dollar project has only 363 million users. In Google+, the +1 button is clicked 5 billion times daily.

Instagram facts

Instagram is a mobile application with 300 million users (53% of them are between 18 and 29 years old). Over 70 million images and videos are uploaded per day. Instagram nicely integrates social and mobile characteristics making it one of the most promising SoLoMo tools in digital marketing.

Pinterest facts

Pinterest has similar characteristics with Instagram, allowing its over 70 million users to pin images they like and not necessarily images they own. Pinterest is more appreciated by women, as 80% of Pinterest users are female. Pinterest offers some amazing online purchase opportunities as 88% of users who pinned a product actually bought it. Recently, Pinterest allowed direct purchases of products from the platform.

Other facts

Finally, we also have to take into consideration the rise of non–English-speaking social networks, operating mainly in China and Russia. Qzone and Wechat in China have 639 and 468 million users accordingly while the Russian VKontake has 100 million users. In addition, there is a growing trend from instant messaging mobile applications with great marketing potentials. WhatsApp counts over 600 million users, Facebook messenger has 500 million users, and Snapchat has already 100 million monthly users in just couple of years of operation. Snapchat's value is close to $20 billion, and many of the big companies are aiming for profitable collaborations.

Social Media's Impact on Society

The primary objective of social networks is to strengthen the social bonds among friends. As such, the social networks became widely known as channels of interpersonal and group communication. The social networking sites have greatly affected the way Internet users are able to communicate with friends, make new friends, get informed, and share links with the public (Boyd and Ellison, 2008). In the traditional ways to communicate, such as the face-to-face interaction, or the phone conversation, new forms of communication have been added.

Nowadays, the Internet users are able to e-mail or IM (WhatsApp, Skype, Viber, etc.) each other as well as initiate a video call. Younger generations consider e-mail and chat as primitive ways to communicate. Twitter posts, Facebook status updates, and Skype conversations are also part of their communication process. In some cases, the Internet users decide to communicate and share their news through online virtual worlds such as the Second Life, or the widely known online games Lineage and World of Warcraft (WoW) with millions of users logging in on a daily basis (Qualman, 2009). Today's Internet users consider themselves as part of an online community, in which popularity is measured by the number of friends, connections, followers they have on Facebook, LinkedIn, and Twitter accordingly.

The online social networks have changed the way people follow the news. Instead of simply getting the news from a newspaper article, or from a TV story, the new generation of Internet users relies heavily on their friends within their network. Users read their Facebook friends' statuses to comment on a news link. The source of the news is not always a traditional newspaper, but also blogs written by anonymous sources. In addition, many mainstream websites covering the news allow their users to comment on their news stories. That leads to the argument that the control is now on the hands of the Internet users who are gradually becoming the gatekeepers of information.

Digital customers are getting more familiar and comfortable with the Internet, and they expect from brands to approach them and interact with them. A website is a portrait of a business, is the beginning of all. Customers may explore in the website and learn about a brand everything they need. Through a website a brand may also provide access to social networks accounts. Social media, like Facebook and Twitter, are becoming the main sources for people's information.

The number of users of social media globally is extremely big. Online profile of a business, product, or service may rise positively in the digital world, in order to manage its purposes. For this reason a new breed of consumer, the SoLoMo consumer, needs to be explored.

The SoLoMo Consumer

This book is an exploration of SoLoMo consumers with a special focus on the generation of Internet users who are having a natural connection with computers and other electronic devices. Prensky (2001) describes digital natives a group of students bearing fundamental distinctions from the classes and generations he had encountered in his academic career. His main argument stems from the observation that these new digital natives seem to have "spent their entire lives surrounded by and using computers, videogames, digital music players, video cams, cell phones, and all the other toys and tools of the digital age" (Prensky, 2001, p. 1).

Digital natives are especially adept at functioning within a web-based interface. Research on this particular characteristic has been widely conducted within market segment research on Gen-Y consumers and products, yet less advanced in academic scholarship on the topic. Studies of the latter sort are generally investigations into socialization rather than contributory to research and development strategies meant to generate profit. In either case, the topic of HRM is tertiary to the broader trends found in the literature.

Gen-Y born after 1980 are children of a digitized world. Change has been rapid. Digital natives in business sectors are especially predisposed to this sociological profile. Configured by e-mail communications, Sharepoint project management, and virtual meetings, digital natives find validation in their professional standing by way of multiple digital accounts, competency in SNS networking, and their ability to forge consensus through self-volition in online forums (CISCO, 2012). Digital natives are first-generation bloggers, wikis, and leaders on Facebook, Linkedin, Twitter, Flickr, etc. Many of those same natives might also have a digital self (also known as avatar) that lives in virtual worlds such as the Second Life or in online games like Lineage and WoW (Qualman, 2009).

These digital natives are equally eager to experience new technological gadgets when they hit the market. The iPhone series and other smartphone phenomenon are evidence of this movement. They listen to music by downloading MP3-formatted songs from the web. They receive information through video streaming applications like YouTube, and they are commenting on anything they found worth discussing. Finally, they even refer to networks to acquire friends. For this new breed of consumers, SoLoMo is not a marketing strategy. It is a way of living.

The next three chapters of this book will explain the characteristics and implications of Social, Local, and Mobile aspects of digital marketing.

CHAPTER 2

#Going_Social

In this chapter you will read:

- Why SoLoMo consumers are social
- Their characteristics of social behavior
- About new trends in social engagement such as social search, visual search, content marketing, and social commerce
- How Twitter, Facebook, and Instagram function as entry points to purchase
- About social entertainment as expressed by the YouTube community, product reviews, home videos, song covers, thumbs up, thumbs down, likes, and dislikes
- How to use collective coupons from deal sites (i.e., Groupon)
- How to seek recommendations through social networks
- A case analysis

Introduction

AdWeek provides an introduction that underlines the inescapable importance of social media as a part of a marketing process.

> *Since 2004, the growth of social media has been near exponential. Back in those days, Facebook—arguably the most mature of the top social networks—only had about 1 million users. By 2011 the network had grown so large; its population was being compared to that of a country. Today, Facebook has more than 1 billion registered users and Mark Zuckerberg has made connecting 5 billion more of a personal mission. Twitter saw steep growth from 2010 to 2012 but according to the infographic, its growth is starting to*

> *slow. Google+ saw the biggest growth of all in 2013, most like because of Google's integration of Google+ into all associated services. If you have a Gmail account, you have a G+ profile. Most recently, Google integrated G+ into YouTube comments. Indeed, Google/Google+ is becoming one big super brand. While there were many holdouts in the earlier days of social media's development, businesses and marketers love social media now. Indeed, 90 percent of marketers are using social media for business, according to the SEJ infographic. Seventy percent have used Facebook to successfully gain new customers and 34 percent have used Twitter to successfully generate leads.*

This chapter introduces the nature of social media marketing from start to finish, in terms of identifying the social nature of consumers in the SoLoMo environment. If there is one hallmark of the social landscape, it is that it is both diverse and fast moving. This chapter examines a plethora of ways that social media has been used to engage customers and how most of that is still very new. The chapter not only introduces all of the different methods in and of themselves, but also gives a sense of best practice by examining the social media approach of the Checkers burger chain. The takeaways for this chapter are that social media is an extremely cost-effective, flexible, and rich way of marketing to customers if approached in the right way, and is the bedrock of a SoLoMo approach.

SoLoMo Consumers Are Social

The growth of the SoLoMo consumer has changed the dynamics of product marketing beyond recognition (Doyle, 2012). The fundamental means by which brands send and receive information, the way that customers make purchasing decisions and find out about products or services, is now completely different.

The main shift has been the change in the information flow dynamic between brand and customer. Before the advent of social marketing, there was a fairly distinct process that most brands went through when marketing a product or service. The first step in the process was to conduct some market research about potential customers, their wants and needs, previous purchasing habits, and so forth. This then allowed the brand to segment their marketing strategy depending on the customers they wanted to talk to and their selected method of engagement. They would then design some marketing collateral to achieve that aim, whether it can be by TV, radio, print advertisement, or whatever. The key is that the brand is in control of the marketing process at all times.

SoLoMo has changed that completely; the brand is not in control of the process, but is merely a participant in a wider array of information sharing and exchange that now determines how people make the decision to buy something (Tuten and Solomon, 2014). There is exceptionally clear evidence to show that people use social engagement to seek recommendations and feedback on brands from people whom they trust, friends or other people in their personal networks whose opinions they trust or believe to be a neutral arbiter. Therefore, people will ask their Facebook friends for recommendations on their purchases, or whether someone has had a good or bad experience at a particular restaurant, for example. Sometimes this is quite passive; someone might simply read that someone has had a great night at a new restaurant, and decide to check it out themselves.

As a wider element of social engagement, websites like TripAdvisor or feedback systems such as those found on eBay have become important parts of the marketing mix. These systems are built around user-generated reviews of products and services, and consumers tend to place a good deal of store in the information that they get from them. Therefore, no marketer can ignore this kind of social engagement and reflexive feedback in their plans. Fundamentally the dynamic has changed so that consumers may now know more about products and services than the marketers themselves; they have the capability to compare and contrast multiple providers very easily, and with no input from the brands themselves.

This means a couple of things for marketers, broadly speaking positive and negative. The positive thing is that consumers can often become very powerful advocates for the brand, much more powerful than the brand itself could be, because they enjoy a level of trust among consumers (Kamins, 2014). Therefore, having a positive engagement strategy that tries to make the most of this—without forcing it—can be extremely powerful. The downside is that if consumers become unhappy with some element of the service, they can amplify their discontent a long way beyond themselves and can cause substantial damage to a brand.

Return on Investment

What really makes SoLoMo sing is the ROI—return on investment. Under traditional advertising models success of a particular campaign is directly correlated to the amount of money put into it. Any form of traditional marketing, be it TV, radio, printed ads, or billboards, requires substantial upfront cost, sometimes many millions of dollars. Moreover, there is no real way of linking that upfront cost to the number of sales derived from it; the ads cost what they cost, and then it is up to the company to make the most of any leads it generates. Social media advertising and particularly SoLoMo have changed that completely (Buhalis and Mamalakis, 2015).

Start-up costs for social media advertising are negligible. The infrastructure is provided by a third party, for example, Facebook, Foursquare, or Twitter, and often it is possible to set up a presence there at no cost at all; there's no charge for setting up a Facebook page or Twitter account. From then, the company can either grow their social media presence organically—at no cost—or use various promoted adverts. Even if they decided to use paid advertising, the cost is directly linked to engagement and the budgets are customizable. In the case of SoLoMo there is often no need to pay for any adverts; the key is in appearing in local search results and similar social offerings, which are part of the essential offer of the social networks anyway. What all of this adds up to is that even the smallest venture can have a widespread social media presence and practice SoLoMo marketing without a huge budget. It is a game changer for many small businesses, because they play on the same basic playing field as larger brands so they can compete more equally (Chan and Yazdanifard, 2014).

Aside from the low cost, what really makes the value of social marketing is the metrics. If you buy an advert in a local newspaper, there are very few metrics that can tell you much about what consumers thought when they saw about it: a general circulation figure of the newspaper, and the number of people who actually contact you as a result. With social media there are huge numbers of metrics available, ranging from basic statistics such as who has seen your page to has actually interacted with it in some way, through geographical overlays of visitors and analytics on how your visitors are connected to other visitors. This means that it is possible to optimize social marketing in a way that is simply impossible with other forms of engagement; and again for small businesses, that kind of data used to be restricted only to big companies (Hoffman and Fodor, 2010). This is a real leveler in marketing terms.

SoLoMo: Now!

What makes this so important for you to engage with now? While it might seem as though all of the techniques of SoLoMo mentioned in this chapter have already been put to work by competitors, we are really only at the beginning of a much larger trend. The technologies that underpin the mobile and social networking elements of SoLoMo are only a couple of years old and people are still figuring out how best to use them. More importantly, people are only now beginning to get enough data on SoLoMo consumer behavior to get an early indication of how consumers are really working with SoLoMo principles. Much of what has been written previously has been based on observations and anecdotes rather than sustained data analysis. As this trend continues to emerge into the future, data analytics and performance trends will become clearer. However, these trends are also being pushed forward by deep technological trends. The rise of the mobile device may give way to wearable tech, and that may have profound changes on the way that people use the SoLoMo principle. It is a fast-moving landscape that marketers need to be constantly monitoring in order to ensure that they are moving in tandem with it.

All of this means that now is the time to build the SoLoMo marketing team in your business, before you get left behind. The conditions are ripe to make the most of the SoLoMo now; the early pioneers have made their mistakes and pointed to the right directions to take, but thier trend as a whole has so much further to go.

New trends in Social Engagement

Social Search

Clearly, in order to make the best out of this social landscape and to use the amplification of social endorsements it is helpful for marketers to have some understanding of how people are connected. There are a several large social networking sites and applications, with many people registered on all of them, and it can be quite difficult being systematic in how to engage with a particular demographic through all of these connections.

Facebook has provided a social search function to developers called the Facebook Social Graph, which is the largest social dataset in the world. Because Facebook is the largest social network in the world, with nearly a billion members, it is in a unique position to track the way that people are connected on different websites and how they use the web (Evans, 2012). This graphs out defined relationships among not just people but other objects such as photographs across websites, so marketers can understand the kinds of webs of relationships that exist and what the potential consequences in engagement are. Google has attempted to create a similar service, though with less success.

The advantage is that marketers can use this to gain a very high-level understanding of the networks that their customers are involved in, and this might open up new opportunities for engagement and expanding reach. It provides a context for all of the other more particular marketing actions that follow, and a loose form of modeling the potential reach.

Content Marketing

One of the interesting behavioral characteristics of social marketing is that customers do not actually respond well to what might be called traditional advertisements, specific advert panels, banners, or text ads that are overlaid on the page; an even worse sin is the pop-up or pop-under advert, as these have largely died out and have little presence in social media. There are various theories advanced for this, but the crux of the matter is that they interfere with the user experience and particularly with the interactions that the consumer is trying to complete with their networks.

Marketers have found a more subtle way of getting their messages through to consumers with the idea of content marketing. This is where content is produced that is designed to look like native content on whatever service the consumer is using. The idea is taken from newspapers, where advertisers often draft adverts to look like the regular editorial content of the paper. The object of the exercise is not to deceive readers as such, but rather to get past their normal defense mechanisms around adverts; once the reader has become engaged by the content then he or she tends to continue reading even as he or she realizes that it is advertising content. Many of you will probably have come across such content at the end of a news article or a blog, where there is a selection of links to "promoted content" or "promoted articles," some with quite unusual headlines.

Deals and Coupons

Deals and coupon sites have had something of a tumultuous ride over the last few years, and in the process have garnered a lot of negative press, but there are still many valid reasons for using such sites as part of a wider social marketing strategy. The key site in this area is Groupon, but there are a number of regional and local sites that need to be considered when working within the SoLoMo principle, but the general principle holds true.

The essential idea of a coupon site is that local businesses can offer a discounted coupon and leverage the traffic of the coupon website to drive their own traffic. This can work particularly well for physical businesses that need to drive people to an actual physical location. The sites initially worked well, but then lost popularity as the fees involved made the transaction unprofitable for coupon issuer and often resulted in disappointed customers when special offers ran out. However, there remain interesting elements of the model that can still be used.

Whatever the short-term profitability of using a coupon service, they remain a very powerful way of generating initial interest in a product or service; the start-up costs of a coupon campaign are relatively modest, and they can generate a lot of traffic very quickly. For those who are looking to create initial exposure for a product or service it can be a very useful tool. Moreover, from the perspective of social marketers, coupons are often very widely shared on social media among certain demographics so the exposure benefits can be greatly amplified even among those who do not necessarily use the coupon itself.

New Behaviors in Social Media

Seeking Recommendations through Social Networks

There is a burgeoning trend in consumers becoming producers in many ways, and creating their own marketing platforms through their own social media and online platforms. There is an increasing trend in people seeking out subscribers, favorites, or followers on whatever platform they have to build their own following; often this is not directly about marketing a product but about building their particular following within a community. Often people can generate very substantial presence within a community, which is very interesting to online marketers.

A good example of this is the world of competitive video gaming. Top players routinely build Twitter and YouTube followers of over 500,000 people, who watch them play and compete in big money tournaments for games such as World of Warcraft, Pro Evolution Soccer, or Fifa. One of the things that brands have sought to do is get these people with large social "capital" to provide direct or subtle endorsements of their products. In the example of competitive gaming, handset manufacturers, seat makers, and headphone designers give freebies to people with large YouTube and streaming followers, so that they are giving implicit endorsements of the products that then encourage their followers to emulate them.

Using Twitter, Facebook, and Instagram as Entry Points to Purchase

Social media has proven a very fertile space to revisit some old tropes in marketing, as it offers a level of engagement that reinvigorates them. Many marketers use the idea of competitions and giveaways on social media as a way of generating an entry point to a purchase; so there is some incentive to engage with the brand. Many of these competitions or giveaways are contingent on some form of purchase, or offer a teaser that should then lead to purchase. The ability to engage with people in an interactive way on social media, and to have a bit of back and forth with them, makes them work very well, as does the limited cost of getting set up in this space.

Embracing the YouTube Community

YouTube has proved an interesting avenue for marketers in general, because videos allow for a multisensory engagement with the user, and they can generally hold the attention of the viewer much longer than other forms of advertisement. The videos themselves can be put to different uses depending on exactly what the marketer is trying to sell, and they can be used either for direct marketing purposes such as product videos or third-party endorsements or some combination thereof. This is best illustrated through a number of examples.

To return to the idea of the competitive gaming industry, many of the top gamers do product review videos or something very similar, such as reviewing their own personal gaming setup, with the intention of promoting certain products. This has worked very well for brands such as BenQ, maker of gaming monitors, as well as Scuf, a maker of bespoke gaming controllers. There are a number of videos on YouTube where players talk through their gaming setup or their championship setup, extolling the technical virtues of these products. Naturally there are many of their fans and aspiring gamers who take note of these videos and buy the same products in order to try and emulate their heroes.

There are also many independent review videos that are popular on YouTube. These people review products or services in a particular niche and give their feedback. The advantage to marketers is twofold; the first is that the cost of collaborating on review video that could accomplish over one million views in a month is a fraction of producing a traditional advertising medium such as a TV spot. Moreover, consumers tend to trust the reviews that they say through these channels because they view them as independent of the brands themselves, and therefore giving honest feedback. With many products and services a video actually allows people to see whatever they are thinking about purchasing in action, which often makes people feel more comfortable with a new thing. It reassures them particularly about whether it does what they think it does, and that it is good value for money.

There are slightly more subtle ways of using YouTube videos to market products. Some marketers have experimented with the idea of spoof cover songs or interview pieces, whereby the putative inventor of something or the "face" of a brand gives an endorsement through the course of an interview. A good example of this is the YouTube campaign that Nestle developed for their Nescafe brand of coffee. They developed a series of YouTube short video adverts that featured a panel discussion with one of their ambassadors George Clooney talking about their social and environmental credentials, and talking up what a sustainable brand Nescafe was. There was never any particular offer during the video, or call to action; it was merely a piece of marketing aiming to fit in with the values of people demographically profiled as likely to view the video which it prefaced.

Social Entertainment

An extension of the idea of these kind of videos is the idea of social entertainment; companies are now developing levels of engagement with their customers through such things as creating games for them to play on their Facebook page. Clearly, there is some distance between playing a game and actually purchasing something from the brand, but the idea is to engage with the customer through something that they enjoy doing and associate with positive thoughts; this then transfers to an extent to the brand. It moves the brand toward a trusted status with people, and makes them more willing to engage with the more direct elements of the marketing plan.

There are other forms of social entertainment such as live video streaming sessions that invite the participation of viewers. To return once again to professional gamers, many have built up larger followers on the sites MLG or Twitch which allow people to watch them play, with an inset screen of the gamer themselves, alongside such features as interactive chatting with the gamers. The gamers physically talk to people in the chat section as they play, giving the whole thing a very interactive feel to it. Typically these gamers now punctuate the play with advertisement breaks that take over the stream for a few seconds, which commercializes what started out as a leisure activity. In addition the stream feeds are overlaid with product promotions. Therefore, the consumers are primarily there for the purposes of entertainment and interacting with their heroes, but it all offers a seamless way of advertising.

Steps Your Business Should Take to Leverage Social Media

The SoLoMo revolution is only in its infancy, so companies and their marketers really need to position themselves for the future right now. There is no right or wrong answer for SoLoMo; it depends on what you are trying to sell and to whom, but there are a couple of things that you can do no matter what industry you are in. You have to set up the right relationship with your customer from the very start; customer experience is the thing that will separate the winners from the losers.

Set up Social Media

It may seem a startlingly obvious thing to say, but it is necessary to sign up to all the social media sites and set each of them up correctly. This can take some time, particularly for those who don't use them personally, but it is worth it. The simple fact is that it is quite likely that consumers are talking about your company, or searching for similar services on social networks, and so it is not really supportable to not involve yourself.

After making the decision to sign up to all of these sites, it is then subsequently necessary to actually manage the social media profiles correctly. There is nothing more off-putting to a potential customer than seeing a social media page that hasn't been updated for 6 months; it suggests a lack of care and a lack of interest in customers. It looks even worse when there are questions or comments from customers that have gone unanswered.

Aside from keeping social media profiles up to date, one of the major management tasks is responding to customer comments, particularly negative ones. A lot of people who run their own business find this a particularly difficult task, because they take the criticism personally and find the customers unreasonable. However, it is an essential task and one that needs to be managed professionally no matter what the size of the company. Generally speaking, the best way of doing this is to have a written policy for engaging with customers that can ensure that everybody knows exactly what to do.

Optimize Websites

It is incredible to say it, but there are still many brands that have a website that is not optimized for mobile devices. Websites that are not responsive to the type of device that they are displayed on, and designed around the strictures of mobile page size and touch screen browsing, are putting customers off in their droves, and their owners probably don't even know it. Opening up a clunky, difficult-to-navigate website on a smartphone is a terrible beginning to the customer experience, and it is very unlikely that it can be recovered.

Therefore, all websites need to be optimized for mobile. The process need not be expensive, because any newly designed web presence will be tailored for mobile, but it is an essential investment. The mobile optimization process might take a little time to complete, since it needs to be very refined around what information customers feed back to you about their site experience. As with any good web design process there should be a culture of testing and refinement based on user data; the opening paragraphs of this chapter noted that the SoLoMo trends is only in its infancy and there will be many changes still to come, so marketers need to be ready to move with this trend.

Design Apps

As important as optimizing websites for mobile users is, it is more important to recognize that most SoLoMo users do most of their browsing through smartphone apps rather than websites per se. According to a recent survey-based report from Forrester Research as mentioned by Sterling (2015), US and UK smartphone owners "use an average of 24 apps per month but spend more than 80 percent of their [in app] time on just five apps." Whether or not it is literally five, this is directionally correct; consumer app time is concentrated in just a few popular apps.

According to the Forrester survey data, which come from a mix of behavioral tracking and self-reporting, Facebook and Google are neck and neck for most mobile-user attention. As it has for some time Facebook owns the top spot, but overall Google is slightly ahead of Facebook given aggregate time spent across Google's portfolio of apps.

Thus, the inescapable conclusion of this is that it is necessary to develop a smartphone app to run on both iOS and Android to ensure that your potential customers can access your business in their preferred manner. This need not break the bank or be overly complicated; app design costs have come down substantially since smartphones were first introduced, so there is no need for an enormous development budget to get something available, and it is essential.

Many companies eschew having an app because they aren't sure what it would do differently to their mobile website, but that is really to miss the point. If you look at many of the most popular apps such as eBay, Twitter, GoogleMail, or Amazon, they do very little that is fundamentally different to their mobile website; there might be the odd trick based on the technical capabilities of the phone itself but nothing central to the point of the app. The reason that apps have been developed is that this is the way that users want to experience the service; apps are a little neater than websites, and they can sync in nicely with things like cameras and photo albums. Consider this:

The Potential of Apps

Those who think they don't need a native mobile app because their site is mobile friendly are missing the huge potential apps have over websites.

> - *When was the last time a customer took a picture of your product with your website?*
> - *When was the last time your website notified a potential customer of a sale as they walked by your shop?*
> - *When was the last time your website told you how a customer felt when they saw your product for the first time?*
> - *When was the last time your site told you the name of that customer who just walked through your shop's door?*

> - *When was the last time your site adjusted the price of an item based on a customer's social influence?*
> - *When was the last time a customer tried your product on, virtually on your site?*
>
> *"Biometrics, geo-location, cameras, sensors, augmented reality, 3D gaming… these are potential game-changers that already exist natively in mobile apps—features you won't find on a traditional website. Not only that, but new functionality that we haven't really thought of is going to be available to apps much sooner than they are for an HTML-based site, if ever. Even if you don't take advantage of those features today, just being on the right platform gets you 80% there."*
>
> (Cristo, 2015)

With a relentless focus on customer experience there is no excuse for not having an app. Apps have an advantage in that it is possible to get better quality analytics from it, because it is essentially a closed environment. Furthermore, the fact that their look and feel is more customizable than a website means it is possible to really polish the user experience and that can really improve engagement with customers. Often the difference between a successful customer experience and a failed one is the last few percent of optimization and testing, not a completely different approach to design (Balakrishnan et al., 2014).

Deals

One of the more difficult elements of marketing in the SoLoMo environment is that it can be quite difficult to get continued engagement from customers; there are so many brands competing in the space, with so many quirky tricks that are trying to attract customers it can be quite difficult to keep customers once you have found them. Too many marketers make the mistake of thinking that acquiring a customer once is the hard part, when in fact keeping them coming back is the real challenge.

Obviously a great user experience and great customer service are the cornerstones of this, but having a system of carefully selected and promoted deals also work very well. There's a number of ways that this can be incorporated into a SoLoMo environment, but broadly speaking it is possible to overlay deals when someone checks in using a social media service. So, for example, if someone were to check in to a restaurant on FourSquare, then they could immediately be offered a 10% discount or a free extra; if someone checks in at a venue on Facebook, they can receive a free upgrade. The possibilities are endless, but the key is that people will know that they need to check in via social media wherever they are in order to access their special offer.

This fulfills all of the SoLoMo criteria; the check-in is through social media; it is localized to a particular venue, and it will almost certainly be done through a mobile device. This is hugely important for marketers, because it ensures that people keep coming back to them on social media sites. One of the key social media metrics is customer churn in engagement; so how many people unsubscribe, unlike, or unfollow a brand over time. Using this kind of deal-based-engagement strategy means that people have to stay somewhat engaged with the brand on social media, affording many other marketing opportunities to them. The check-in approach usually also reveals a large amount of information about the user, such as their essential personal details, previous check-ins, friends, activity, and so on. All of this can be put to the use of the marketer.

Case Study

Checkers (www.checkers.com) (and sister brand Rally's) are the largest operator of double drive-in burger restaurants in the United States. They focus on a fast-food offering of high-quality hamburgers, French fries, milkshakes, and hot dogs. They work the SoLoMo principle in a number of different ways depending on the service, but it has contributed in large part to them being one of the fastest growing fast-food chains in the county with over 700 outlets. Their marketing requirements are quite complex because, although in theory they have the same menu in all of their fast-food restaurants, they need to accommodate the requirements of all of their franchisees; not all restaurants might be participating a particular offer item. Furthermore, they are in a fiercely competitive market and they need to be able to develop a rapport with customers beyond that of other local eateries wherever they have a presence.

Mobile Site and Application

Checkers has both a mobile-optimized website and an app available on Google and Android. Both of these are extremely simple, because they are geared almost entirely around helping the user find their nearest branch. On both services the GPS beacon of the site is used, or a zip code, to push the user toward their closest branch. There are a few other elements to the mobile site and app such as the menu, but they are not designed to be engagement tools on their own. Interestingly they do contain links to all of the social media properties of the company.

Facebook

Checkers adopt an innovative strategy for their Facebook marketing because they operate independent pages for each of their stores rather than one page for the whole group. They do this so that people can engage with the store that is closest to them usually, or they can check in to an individual branch of Checkers. The individual pages are used to market special offers from each store.

From the point of view of Checkers and their individual franchisees this is an extremely cost-effective form of marketing. The capture above shows a typical restaurant that has almost 2,000 people who like the page for that restaurant, and then have the special offers visible on the page placed into their regular Facebook timeline. There are almost no other means by which an individual franchisee could regularly target the same 2,000 people whom they know quite a lot about, and whom they know are geographically very proximate to their branch. Furthermore, the high rating of the restaurant by those 2,000 "likers" (4 out of 5 stars) is visible very prominently on the page, and gives the restaurant a large degree of trust among potential new customers. These rating are given by customers rather than the company itself, and they can have a dramatic effect on the visitor rate of the company. What is really important to understand is that the SoLoMo principle has allowed this kind of engagement to be achieved for a single franchise of a much larger chain. This kind of hypertargeted marketing based on location and social media is the hallmark of the new age of online marketing.

FourSquare

As a company Checkers has used FourSquare as a core pillar of its SoLoMo marketing, at the group level rather than individual franchisees. They have set up a special offer whereby people who check in *regularly* receive a special free gift—at the time of writing they get a free shake on every third check-in—and they have advanced bonuses for people who check in the most; those who become the "Mayor" of a Checkers branch through being the person who has checked in the most at that branch gets a free small shake on every visit. This, again, is a quintessential example of SoLoMo marketing. It is social because it can only be activated through a third-party social media app; it is local because it is aggregated around visits to individual locations, and it is mobile because the check-ins can only be completed via a mobile device.

What makes this particularly interesting is that the rewards are structured around regular social media interactions. One-off check-ins won't achieve very much for the customer, because they don't achieve very much for Checkers. Checkers wants to get people into the habit of regular engagement with the company on social media, so its FourSquare strategy is built around engendering that repeated local interaction with the company.

Twitter

The company uses Twitter in a different way to its other social media platforms, but in a very intelligent way. There are a smattering of special offers and promotional tweets, but in the main the twitter feed is used for engaging with customers, in one of two ways. First, the company is very proactive in responding to customer questions through the Twitter feed—restaurant openings, queries about ingredients, customer service comments, product enquiries, and so on. The second is that the company likes to "retweet" and otherwise share the tweets of customers at individual locations.

Thus, they engender a level of engagement with people through the SoLoMo principle. People use their smartphone to take a picture of what they are eating and where, and then this is often retweeted or replied to by the company as a whole. This combines all of the elements of local, mobile, and social and gives the company a friendly, approachable demeanor in the eyes of its customers.

Summary

Checkers give a very good example of how to use the SoLoMo principle as part of a customer acquisition and engagement strategy. The sections above noted how they used various social media platforms to promote sustained engagement with their brands through localized special offers and promotions. Each individual component of the SoLoMo approach that Checkers use is relatively self-explanatory, but it is worth reflecting on the strategy as a whole.

The social media campaign as a whole is very well planned because the purpose of each social platform is very well thought out. They haven't simply established a presence on each social media platform and then dealt with whatever comes their way through it, they have a specific purpose for every single one of the social media platforms that they use. Twitter is for customer questions and engagement, Facebook localizes the offers to specific groups, FourSquare drives regular social media check-ins, and the mobile app and website drive people to the stores. In many ways this is the key lesson of the Checkers example to take forward into a SoLoMo practice of your own.

There are bewildering array of social media platforms and a bewildering array of different approaches to them. In that lies a danger; there is a risk that brands simply sign up to every social media platform around with no clear vision of what they are trying to achieve from them all, or whether they actually fit in with a SoLoMo strategy. In order to make a SoLoMo strategy work, or indeed any social media strategy, there needs to be a very clear rationale behind every single platform in use (Motameni and Nordstrom, 2014). As Checkers show, if this is done correctly it can be a hugely powerful way of marketing particularly when considered from the perspective of return on investment (Armstrong et al., 2014).

Conclusion

This chapter has demonstrated what social marketing means in terms of SoLoMo and ways of engaging customers. This chapter has covered a lot of different topics aimed at introduced various mechanisms of engagement that have been used in social media marketing ranging from coupons to video endorsements. Not all of these topics will be relevant to every single reader or every single industry sector, but it is important to have a very good understanding of how social media has been used to engage with customers so that you can choose the right mode for your circumstances.

The chapter demonstrated some social media best practice from the Checkers burger chain, and noted how that linked in to their SoLoMo campaign. The Checkers example underlined a number of key lessons for the chapter as a whole to be taken into the following chapters on more applied topics. The first is that while there are many routes to social engagement it is necessary to have a plan for how they will all come together in a social marketing campaign. Second is that it is not sufficient to simply sign up to social media sites; there has to be a commitment and management practice involved in keeping them all up to date.

Most importantly, this chapter has underlined how fast moving this social media marketing space is, and how one of the key challenges is keeping up to date with all of the different strands as they evolve. The only certain thing is that marketers cannot sit on the sidelines and watch, they need to become involved in all of this and make social a core part of their customer engagement and marketing approach.

CHAPTER 3

#Staying_Local

In this chapter you will read:

- Why SoLoMo consumers are local
- Their characteristics of local behavior
- About Geosocial networking
- New trends in GeoLocation services
- How to use GeoSocial applications
- About online payments
- How to use coupons
- How to use beacons
- About the benefits of geolocation services

Introduction

Firms need to think Local. Of course, national brands have a bigger budget to spend than what a small business has, but consumers nowadays look for local businesses that can fix their problems and fill their needs. Affinity and proximity create the kind of top-of-mind awareness that drives sales and create a guaranteed success. In this chapter the authors will analyze the second characteristic of the SoLoMo consumer, which is "staying local." Consumers are submitting more and more location data, with the use of geolocation techniques (Eugen et al., 2014). Social networks, such as Foursquare and Google Places, use these data of information in order to connect and coordinate users with local people or events that match their interests in the highest possible degree. In this chapter the authors are going to extensively analyze the following topics: new trends in geoLocation services, geosocial networking, use of geolocation applications (such as Foursquare) to check in, and finally payments, beacons, and coupons.

By using SoLoMo strategies firms could convince people walking to their store simply by offering a check-in deal on Facebook or Foursquare. Basically consumers are getting attracted to the store by the offer (i.e., Foursquare), but at the same time the store is connected in the mind of the consumer with a trusted online platform. If consumers trust an online social media platform and see an offer or a discount in that platform, subconsciously they trust the business.

Keep in mind that using a SoLoMo strategy is like using an integrated system. The different elements cannot maximize the value of the SoLoMo strategy if they are implemented separately. Small businesses cannot afford to underestimate the role SoLoMo plays in today's purchasing decisions. Its ability to tap into networks of customers is probably the greatest unused marketing opportunity in existence.

SoLoMo Consumers Are Local

The Local marketing is the final element of the SoLoMo (Social, Local, and Mobile) marketing strategy. Consumers are adopting new technologies and social media interfaces that allow them to behave in a different way from how they did in the past. Nowadays consumers have more power. The new consumers do not waste time going through the traditional distribution channels through which their level of control was extremely low. Now, they are experimenting with new channels through which their voice can be heard. The key search engine companies have realized this new era, and they are trying to adopt it.

For example Google, which is the most prominent search engine, is changing their search algorithm in order to emphasize more on local results when it comes to search queries of consumers. Google did this because they recognized the new trend of the consumers which is to take action when they search for something over the Internet, so the results are now based more on local solutions. Through the new features of Google plus, the consumers now have great power when it comes to decide on a product or service that has been consumed by their friends on Google Circles. Through Google+ consumers could check trusted reviews all across Google. They could find out about new places close to them and can decide based on the recommendations of their friends.

Google gives the opportunity to the consumers to give precise ratings and provide with comments in order to help other consumers to make fast decisions.

Although Google is important, firms need to make sure that they do not overlook the other search engines and social platforms. It is extremely important to use consistent and complete information. Another company that publishes crowd-sourced reviews about local businesses and is extremely popular is Yelp. Yelp had an average of approximately 139 million monthly unique visitors in the third quarter of 2014 and more than 67 million local reviews have been posted. According to a Nielsen survey (2014), 80% of the people who use Yelp visit the website before spending money, and 93% of those say that visiting Yelp leads to a local purchase. When the consumers were asked to rank the factors that help them find local business they replied that the leading factor is the reviews (44%), followed by ratings (26%), number of reviews (17%), and reviews written by someone they know (14%). The most common businesses that were searched on Yelp.com, according to the same study, are the restaurants, followed by beauty and spa, food, nightlife, home and local services and professional services. Other businesses commonly searched on Yelp included hotels and travel, auto, arts and entertainment, health and medical, real estate, and financial services.

The top three motivations for consumer to use location-based apps are receiving a coupon or deal, to learn more about the location, and to meet up with friends. Firms should try to incorporate all of these three elements in their apps. They should design their campaigns in order to offer an overall experience and not just another coupon or offer. An example of that realization from the firms' side is Foursquare. They tried to reposition and rebrand the app and tried to separate the check-in and the location-based searching, because they realized that not all consumers want to check in wherever they go but they want to use the benefits of the geosocial networking. Foursquare's recent separation of these two features was very smart as they can now target those who enjoy checking in and those who want to search within their location without to worry about privacy issues. The rebranding clearly came from the new needs of the consumers.

Characteristics of SoLoMo Consumers' Local Behavior

The SoLoMo consumers have some unique characteristics and that is why they have to be treated in a different way than the ordinary consumers. Firms need to realize the huge potential that technology is offering. By understanding these unique characteristics and by engaging them into a solid strategy that could create an unforgettable experience to the consumer. The Social aspect drives traffic (online and offline), the Local aspect drives action, and last but not least the Mobile aspect drives the opportunity.

As opposed to just a few years back, nowadays consumers have at their disposal an immense amount of information just by using their smartphones. They could easily check at any time and no matter where they are reviews and ratings about the products or services that they are interested in. They could also compare prices from different online and offline retailers; in order to find the lowest price, they could check the inventory and then proceed to the actual buy. If they want, they could also share their retail experiences and potential purchases with their friends through social media platforms.

The SoLoMo consumers, due to their unique nature, could be characterized as hyperconnected shoppers who constantly demand a more personalized experienced. Since they are sharing every single bit of information with the retailers, they expect in return to receive products that meet their exact needs and wants. Retailers need to understand that for the information they receive from the consumer, they should give them back something extremely personalized. That is something that most firms have not realized yet. They believe that consumers are sharing their information just because they want occasionally to receive a discount and that is more than enough to them. With the amount of information that is received, firms are able to perform marketing communication campaigns in a more efficient way and are able to target their audiences with a quite high success rate.

Without doubt, the most effective strategy in order to get, keep, and grow your customers while increasing their satisfaction and thus customer loyalty is to always be available to your customers. One of the main characteristics of the SoLoMo consumers is that they constantly seek that availability from the retailers they are interested in. They want to be able to interact with their favorite retailers 24/7. And the retailers must be there for them. Another characteristic of the local behavior of the SoLoMo consumer is that they constantly seek a way to interact with the retailers, not only through one social media platform.

SoLoMo consumers are using more than one platform in order to shop. That means that the retailers need to constantly engage with the consumers through various platforms and they should be consistent when they do that. That means that they should have the same type of information in every communication channel. For example, when the firm is mentioning the address of the shop, either through a pinpoint in their website or through Foursquare, they need to make sure that these two location match 100%. In many cases simple but yet crucial information, as the address of the shop, could confuse the consumers. Furthermore another characteristic of their local behavior is that this new breed of consumers is more acceptable to new mobile apps and SMS campaigns. However, localization is a low-hanging fruit opportunity for optimal SoLoMo strategies, by creating relevant assortments, marketing campaigns, and offers for specific stores and geographic areas. Retailers must not interact with the consumers if they do not have to offer something relevant to their needs.

Locality maybe one of the most difficult aspects in terms of implementation. It is the most difficult, simply because in an online environment the retailers are asked to provide a physical location. As much as we try to offer an online experience we must face the truth! Local stores are where the most important experiences will always happen. Even the world's largest online retailers have started realizing this and have begun experimenting with pop-up physical stores. The physical experience is going to close the sale. That sale of course might not take place in the physical store, but it could take place online. In those stores consumers can touch and feel a product before making a purchase, or even ask questions about the product to one of the employees. Brands that really want to stay in touch do so across all channels, not separately within each channel.

Geosocial networking

With the use of geolocation technology every company is able to obtain information in real time and locate a mobile device (which is connected to the Internet) on the map with quite high level of accuracy at any given point in time. The information of the user could be collected through various ways such as GPS technology and cellular data information, credit card transactions, tags in photographs, and postings on social networks. It is an undisputable fact that geolocation technology has become the basis of every location-aware application on a mobile device.

From the firms' perspective the geolocation data could be used in many different ways. They can be adjusted to the needs of the firm, and they could serve as starting point of the interaction between the consumer and the firm. The communication touch point becomes virtual. The localization of delivered content and the enforcement of access, which is based on geographic location, is definitely one of the main elements that firms are using nowadays. Along with this overflow of information some main security issues arise. Questions like "What type of information should be collected?" or "How often it should be collected?" are issues that puzzle not only the firms but also the users. There is an antithetical point of view from the part of the consumers. They want to have as much information as they can get, but at the same time they do not want to share their own information with other users. Therefore, it is imperative for businesses to be aware of issues that have to do with privacy, in order to be in position to use the geolocation technology in the best possible way.

Firms have in their disposal two main ways to gather geolocation data, and these are the "active way" and the "passive way." In the active way the collection of geolocation data is performed through the GPS chip and/or through the cellular data. In the passive way the collection of geolocation data is performed through other third-party geolocation service providers or through a correlation with stored databases obtained from purchase records and user-provided information.

In order for firms to be able to build a sustainable relationship and maximize the value of each consumer they need to understand the privacy issues that users are having. They should respect their boundaries when it comes to the use of location-based information. The message that comes through geolocation services should be delivering the maximum experience to the user. That means it should be relevant and engaging in order to increase the possibilities of creating a well-established relationship that will lead to increased profitability. If a firm is overdoing it with location-based messages, then the user is going to start ignoring the messages even if they are targeted to a very specific group. The key of the success is for the firms to be transparent and to make the consumers understand the ways they are going to use the information that they share with them.

Geolocation data generally are used for three purposes:

1. Georeferencing is basically used by the firms in order to obtain the location of a user and to put that information in a map. That information could be viewed live, or it could be stored for future reference.
2. Geocoding is when information about a place stored on a map, and then this information is shared with other users, for example, when a user is trying to find a hotel that offers very specific facilities.
3. Geotagging, is basically adding geographic information to usually a photograph and being able to send that photograph with all the information attached to it.

Geosocial networks are definitely winning grounds in our everyday life, but still consumers are not ready to use their full potential. By now consumers are used to build connections to other consumers online. They feel quite comfortable to connect with someone they have not met in the past and to share information over the Net. Consumers do not even think twice before they share their information to strangers. Of course doing this in real life is something completely different. Consumers, due to their introvert nature, are still not ready to start conversation with somebody who they tracked, through their app, in the couch next to them.

A few years ago social media interfaces were asking their users to write down their status and what they have been up to. This level of interaction is considered to be outdated. Nowadays the users could easily upload the place they are into and share it with their group of friends. In this way the users could let their friends know where they are, or to find places that people that they know have recommended. At the same time they can use this service in order to remotely check in at clubs, bars, and restaurants. So basically geolocation is the process of finding, determining, and providing the exact location of a mobile phone or any other networking device. It enables device location based on geographical coordinates and measurements.

The GPS of the phone is using satellite data in order to calculate the exact position of the user. When a GPS signal is unavailable, geolocation apps can use information from cell towers or even from Wi-Fi networks. In this way the geolocation app on the users' phone can spot the position fairly accurately. The main problem with the GPS technology is that it does not work accurately inside buildings. For example, inside a shopping mall geolocation apps cannot make use of GPS technology. In that case users should check in manually from within the app interface. Eventually, though, more-advanced GPS systems should increase the accuracy of geolocation positioning inside buildings.

The geolocation apps are designed, on the one hand, to report the location of the user to other users, and, on the other hand, they associate real-world locations (such as restaurants and events) to the users' location. Since the majority of the SoLoMo consumers use a smart mobile device, more and more data are being collected and then shared to other SoLoMo users. Geolocation applications could also run in a desktop, but you do understand that as they run in a mobile device they create a far richer experience because all the data change according the change of the location of the user.

New Trends in Geolocation Services

Sometimes when consumers use an app on their smartphone, the app asks from them permission to identify the location of the phone. Actually for some apps that is imperative and they do not work otherwise. When a person uses an app on their smartphone, the app may ask for permission to access the location data of the phone. In most of these apps (especially in the free versions) they are lots of ads that all belong to the advertising network close to location of the phone. By using this method your firm could easily target through advertising a very specific group of consumers. This extremely targeted local advertising message is tailor-made to the consumer's special interest and location. This hyper-local marketing strategy is used by Amazon. Amazon segments the market by location and sends e-mails to user, by pointing out offers close to their location.

In the USA, the majority of national brands are expected to increase or maintain their local marketing budget for the next few years. This shows that firms have actually started realizing the real potential of the SoLoMo strategy. Especially small firms need to take advantage of the new location-based trend and thus skyrocket their profits. Of course small firms do not have the resources to compete with big corporations, but the only thing they need to do is to make sure that the consumers are aware of every single place (online and offline) where they could interact with the firm. Many times firms are concentrating only in the online touch points and forget all about the offline. Only the synergy of both online and offline could create a holistic approach for the SoLoMo consumer.

Of course not all online media could be used with an extreme ease. In many cases firms need to seek the help of an expert in order to optimize their online marketing assets so as the search engines locate the content of the website. With this technique (search engine optimization) the firms maximize the potential of their online content. During the last years most of the firms have established an online presence. In many cases firms are not paying attention to the mobile friendliness of their website. The website should be able to adapt when it is accessed by a mobile device (tablet or a smartphone), because the SoLoMo consumers are using only this type of devices when they perform their online research and online shopping.

Of course being local means that the firm needs to be aware of "what is out there." They need to be extremely focused when it comes to the monitoring of their brand over the Internet but as well as the monitoring of the consumer. Through the various social media channels the firms should be able to gather all the information about their brands. Good comments or bad comments should be equally welcomed because they provide useful information about the future success of the brand. Of course the firms are not performing brand and consumer monitoring only for their brand but also about the market and the competition. It is an unofficial type of market research which is updated constantly. This could be accomplished through the use of free online tools like Social Mentions or even Google Alerts. Another way for firms to have a more successful local marketing approach would be to experiment with location-based services such as Yelp, Foursquare, Tinder, Gowalla, Groupon, Google Places, etc.

The new trends in geosocial networks expand in every sector, since all firms no matter their size have realized the necessity of using this method in order to approach their consumers. A very recent trend in geosocial networks is that of "food sourcing." When consumers enter a restaurant they could not check in only themselves but also their orders. They could also choose the extra ingredients they desire in their food and award points for every selection. In order for restaurants to support and enhance this new trend they award their customers by giving them discounts and coupons.

Another trend in geosocial networking has to do with "freelancing networks." These networks serve the purpose of allowing users to find new job opportunities. Users set up a profile, and they are allowed to connect with future employers and employees. Mood sourcing is becoming a must in between the geolocation application. With mood sourcing the user could check in not only his location but also his mood. In order to do that they use prefixed emoticons or text (Feeling Happy☺). "Stuck" and "Pocket Life" are two examples of mood sourcing geosocial networking. Pocket Life also has integration with Facebook through an app and has its own social networking features.

Firms have realized the real potential not only of online shopping and the benefit that they add to online personality of the brand but to the offline as well. For that reason they should take advantage of the "social shopping." With this geosocial networking service users are able to create their own unique profiles and collect information for different brands they find online and offline. Usually when a user buys or sees something that has already bought or would like to buy, they post it on a social media platform (Facebook or Instagram) in order to check the reactions of their friends. With the use of a geosocial network app users are able to download images of the products that they are interested in and share it with their friends, without taking pictures. This is an extremely useful feature and online retailers need to affiliate with geosocial networks, even to the extent of giving commissions to them. Some retailers have installed sensors in their retail shop so they can track if the users are physically in their shop (because they could also check in remotely) and give to those users more offers and promotions.

Another technology firms can use is "geofencing." Basically by employing that strategy the firm is creating a virtual bubble around the physical location of the business. Within that range people are going to receive notifications if they have opted to receive messages from the firm. By using geofencing apps business could just ping a deal to anyone who follows them on Facebook and happens to be in their neighborhood.

As for how businesses can use location-based apps, the future lays in the development retail mapping. It will be interesting to see how retail mapping will play out, and to see the future of location-based apps in general. As users become more and more accustomed to the use of smartphones, undoubtedly the future of location-based apps will change. More and more users of smartphones are taking them with them on their trips. Especially if the trip is a shopping trip, then an app like Shopkick is going to give them another level of experience. Apps like that are typically location-based rewards program where consumers get points for just walking in the store.

Use of Geosocial Applications to Check in

There are two basic types of location-based services. The first type is the one that is accumulating users' information (based on location) and provides those aggregated information to other users, and the second type is the geosocial services that let users "check in" to specific locations and at the same time allows them to share that with their friends. In the beginning geosocial apps were using one type or another, but nowadays most geosocial apps combine those two types. With almost all geosocial apps users could "check in" and provide information about their location, and at the same time they could provide information about their activities in the shared location. Seventy-four percent of adult smartphone users get directions or any other type of information based on their current location.

Nowadays users do not want only to know where you are but what you are doing in that place. Foursquare is a perfect example of this duality. Foursquare, as a geosocial service, was originally aiming at users who just wanted to share with their friends their location. The 12% of adult smartphone users use a geosocial service such as Foursquare to "check in" to certain locations or share their location with friends. The system originally was based on collecting points, and every time the user was checking in at the same place, he was earning more points. That was of course serving only the purpose of sharing location. Foursquare very soon realized that users wanted something more than that. For that reason they incorporated into the system real-time location-triggered suggestions, activities, and recommendations that could be shared with friends as long as with other users. For example, when a user enters a retail shop, Foursquare sends a push notification saying "Your friends loved this offer." These push notifications, since they are coming from a trusted source, are prompting the user the check out the same offer that their friends saw earlier. After the great success of Foursquare almost all major social media incorporated the function of location. Facebook, Instagram, and Twitter have added an optional location services. Some other social media platforms are using Foursquare so that users could send their location and share their information about the place that they have checked in.

The most common geolocation service users are engaging with is Facebook and then Foursquare followed by Google Plus. Instagram and Yelp are not being used so often for "check-in" purposes.

With the increased use of geolocation services, many social media platforms are providing to the user the option to automatically "tag" their updates with the current location they are in. Almost one-third of the social media platform users, in the USA, have enabled this option in their accounts. People of age group under 50 live in suburban areas are more likely to use the new trend of automatic geolocation tagging. These trends show the ascent of location awareness and the role it might play in the life of users as well as the technology companies that are striving to provide more alert-style applications that are able to tell people who and what is near them. Local is a bigger part of the broader social media landscape, and the rise of local services is strongly tied to the increase in smartphone ownership.

On the other hand, over 33% of smartphone users have turned off the location tracking on their phones, or they allow only to specific applications to have access to it. At the same time most of those users have tried to access information, provided by other users, in a geolocation app. These users are concerned about their privacy, but at the same time they would like to have access to other people's information. This paradox is quite evident in today's online environment. Users want to remain anonymous, but at the same time they want to have access to the information that other user provides. The numbers do change a bit when it comes to teenagers. Almost half of them (under 17) have turned off the location services on their phones not because they worried about other people or companies being able to access that information but because they do not want their parents to know where they are.

There is a growing trend throughout the world concerning the country of origin effect. Country of origin serves as a cue from which consumers make inferences about product and product attributes. The country of origin cue triggers a global evaluation of quality, performance, or specific product attributes. Consumers infer attributes to the product based on country stereotype and experiences with products from that country. That is something that local stores should take under consideration. For example, there is a big movement which is called "Made in the USA" and is basically urging the consumers to buy local food. Basically the aim of this movement is to make consumers buy food and vegetables that was grown close to their houses.

That is all about the locality of the SoLoMo strategy. Firms should take advantage of this local trend and should provide customers with better local discounts and coupons. That will initiate the first interaction and will probably lead to a fruitful relationship.

Payments

One of the most exciting trends of geolocation services is that of payments. As explained previously smartphones either through GPS or through mobile data could have access to the location of the user. Smartphones recognize the place the users are located in and make the payment without even the users to touch their phones. Any business could accept mobile payments no matter their location by using this type of technology. The most successful app that performs geolocation payment is "Wallet." Through the app, the smartphone of the user automatically detects the exact location, through a check-in feature, but also in some cases the user could also do a manual check-in. The user could buy a product or a service and through the Wallet integration with the app used by the employees, the payment is done without even taking the phone out of his or her pocket.

Similar examples of this geo payment trend can be found in transportation apps such as "myTaxi." The app myTaxi recognizes your arrival at the destination previously specified by yourself and undertakes the payment just with a simple confirmation, after both driver and passenger see a confirmation that they have arrived to the destination, as well as the final cost of the ride.

More and more users have started paying by using geolocation services, and it has raised some security concerns. According to big financial and credit firms geolocation not only helps give the consumer more relevant offers but also prevents fraud because it links the payment with the physical check-in of the consumer. Most firms believe that geolocation payment adds an incremental value to the consumers which will be essential for digital wallet adoption to grow. Basically that will happen because it is far easier to tap than to swipe. Of course some researchers stress out the fact that it is easy enough to swipe a physical card so there are no obvious benefits to replacing that with tapping or scanning a phone. So they argue that geolocation payments are trying to solve a problem that does not exist. That is why firms need to focus more on the benefits of the security that these type of payments offer.

Use of Coupons

The location-based mobile coupon services are becoming more and more popular not only to the users but also to the firms since they have understood the full benefits that could have from them. With the use of coupons marketers can upload the store location that participates in any coupon promotions. When users are in close proximity to the store, they could receive notification that will remind them that they have a coupon for that specific store. This type of reminder has proven to be of great success, and it does increase the gross sales of the store. In many cases coupons could include a list of nearby participating locations. In addition to that they could give the consumers very easy access on the information regarding the specific store. From the business perspective, when consumers are using coupons, it is tremendously easy for the firm to track down information about the user.

Undoubtedly location-based marketing offers great potential not only to the consumers but also to the firms. It has been characterized as a way of joining together people, places, and media. Firms are in a position to know the current location of their consumers, and also their history. By taking advantage of such information firms are able to give the users more-relevant, timely content experience. Although firms have this great power, they should not treat their brands carefully. If they collect this huge amount of information but at the same time fail to give back to the consumers a valuable experience, the consumers could just disable the location sharing or could just delete the app.

Use of Beacons

The location technology should be thoroughly understood by the firm. The three great advantages that offers are presence, history, and proximity. These three key aspects enable the brand to deliver a spot-on targeted message in the most relevant time and place and at the same time to achieve extremely high levels of engagement. That is the dream of every marketer!

Since geolocation services do not work in the optimum way inside a building, firms need to deploy the technology of beacons. This type of technology enables firms to track their customers within a matter of inches (microlocation). This offers a great advantage because firms could precisely locate someone within a big retail shop and offer real-time experiences to their customers. Market research companies used to deploy a bunch of researchers inside the stores in order to observe the movements of the consumers. There is no need for those now because consumers willingly provide that information to the firm. Knowing the exact parts of the shop that the consumers are going around provides a huge benefit to the firm. Since they have that information, they can send follow-up messages to a targeted audience.

In addition to the targeted messages, firms could also use microlocation in order to know the exact location of the consumer inside the shop. By doing that, they could potentially guide them through and help them locate products inside the store. Basically they could offer corridor-to-corridor directions inside the retail shop. Their loyalty cards could just pop up along with personalized barcoded coupons that they could use in the cashier scanner.

Benefits of Geolocation Services

The benefits of geolocation for the businesses are applicable to almost every single sector (i.e., retailing, financial services, transportation, etc.). Along with the increased supply of location-based apps (from the firms' side) there is an increased consumer demand for more apps. The users have understood that they benefit as well by sharing their information with the firm as well as with other users.

One of the main benefits of geolocation apps from the firms' perspective is that the advertising is extremely targeted. Since the marketing budget is getting more and more shrunk, the marketing managers need to spend it wisely. With the use of geolocation data firms are able to advertise their brands in very specific areas in order to maximize the effectiveness of the communicational campaign. In addition to that firms are able to understand more deeply the needs and wants of the consumers and are able to have an understanding of customer requirements and expectations for their brands.

Another major benefit for firms is that they could customize the content as well as the delivery of a service plus they could achieve a better asset management. Firms could easily gather information about the actual but also about their prospect clients in order to be able to approach them in the future. Other examples for the use of geolocation services could be highway toll devices, vehicle ad hoc networks (that are used for emergency), etc.

Companies do recognize the benefits of "geomarketing" and that of the apps that give discounts and promotions directly to the user, when they purchase a product or a service, providing real-time and extremely valuable information about the customer preferences. Otherwise, in order for firms to acquire such data they would have to invest huge amounts of money in marketing research. Since the budget of the marketing department is constantly getting lower, firms should make use of these services in order to collect data. These data could provide information on key market trends, or integrated into a customer profile to provide a more personalized experience. Without the geolocation services this type of real-time information would be extremely difficult to be collected. On the other hand, users do benefit in a great degree. By using the geolocation service they could receive information that is relevant to their purchases. They could also receive information about offers and discounts in relevant shops that are nearby their location.

Geolocation service is definitely the future of businesses. This type of technology could be used in combination with other online platforms and provide an immense amount of information regarding the consumers. This information will be used in order for firms to create an online as well as offline fully customized experience.

CHAPTER 4

#Being_Mobile

In this chapter you will read:

- The new mobile era
- The mobile consumer
- Mobile consumer behavior
- SoLoMo is mobile
- Multiscreen and multitask behavior
- Mobile marketing strategy

Introduction

Nowadays there are more than 2 billion smartphones in use worldwide. The world communicates regularly through mobile and is given the opportunity to have access to a vast range of information anytime, anywhere. It is also the way for digital marketers to connect and communicate with consumers. An interesting proportion emerges from Econsultancy's briefing that an average 16% of revenue comes from mobile and 20% of sales are influenced by mobile engagements (Econsultancy, 2014).

The contemporary way of living requires innovation, meaning anything old or dissatisfying should be replaced by something new and easy-going. Mobile phones changed the physical and social environment. So anyone of us can be in person in one place and can communicate with another person who is cited in another location. And this location can be physical or digital or even virtual. The fact that people can carry Internet wherever they go creates a feeling that they can be everywhere at the same moment. It is obvious to marketers that human behavior differentiates in digital and physical space, even though it is the same person who exhibits these different behaviors or even personalities. It is true: The communication environment influences the actual environment (Yamamoto, 2010).

A mobile phone offers its owner freedom. This freedom derives from the fact that they can involve in doing many different functions: making a call, texting, browsing the Internet, e-mailing, doing the shopping, and socializing. Mobiles incorporated their potentials also in order to facilitate everyday activities without cashier, for example, paying bills, accessing Internet banking, etc. Also people tend to customize their mobiles in order to better match their personalities. Most importantly, a mobile phone is a reassurance in case of an emergency that provides a feeling of safeness. Mobiles have brought in our lives a new culture. Face-to-face communication is replaced to a great degree with digital communication. The concepts of place and time are now substituted with anywhere, anytime (Yamamoto, 2010).

People around the globe want at the same time individuality, uniqueness, and involvement in a certain community whose members share common characteristics. Since mobile communication became more convenient and inexpensive, mobile users consider their mobile devices extension of their hands. Therefore, marketers are benefiting from this situation by accessing consumers anywhere and almost anytime.

The new consumer easily accepts anything that is considered technologically advanced. Regarding the purchase of a product or service, consumers conduct their customized "marketing research" on the Internet by collecting information, attributes, and prices. The manufacturer in order to keep in touch with consumer's demands should have a strong Internet presence; hence, the interaction between the two counterparts is more vivid than ever. Marketers must be alert and keep up with the rapidly changing environment. Consumers are able to obtain information and read reviews or even complaints with a single click. Positive opinions or negative word of mouth can be easily spread (Yamamoto, 2010). This situation is both a blessing and a curse for the marketing world. Nevertheless, businesses have the opportunity to promote and sell their products through an e-shop, without investing large amounts of money on a brick-and-mortar store.

Consumer behavior has shifted from a passive consumer to a new breed that is seeking information, reading and learning, participating, and cocreating. New technologies contributed to a large degree to the emergence of the new consumer (Shiffman, 2008). This new type of consumer is in pursuit of creativity and fresh ideas that will solve his or her problems and will satisfy his or her needs and, in the end will, create value (The Economist, 2007).

In the digital era a lot is said about the mobile consumer, who is seeking information for a tangible or intangible product using his or her mobile device. The mobile consumer is a person who likes using technology through which he or she gathers information, is not always concerned about brand loyalty or trust, considers social sharing is more important than the corporate organization, and adopts attitudes according to his or her age or social status.

Mobile Behavior

In our days mobile phone devices are primary communications and media tools. Let's take a quick look of the mobile behavior in UK: 2 out of 3 adults own a smartphone and checking it an average 150 times a day (Mobile Marketing Association, 2013). Also 2 out of 3 smartphone and tablet users say mobile has meaningfully changed the way they shop. McKinsey's (2013) research on mobile habits in the UK suggests it should be based on a simple principle: providing a fast, easy, enjoyable shopping experience. They want clean, mobile-optimized sites with easy-to-read pages that load quickly, easy-to-use shopping carts, and smooth checkouts. In order to understand the mobile consumer it is crucial to first get an insight of the differences within the generations and their characteristics. This is an initial step of segmenting the mobile consumers.

Generations

The lifestyle of *Generation X* (born 1960 and after) demonstrates significant differences compared to previous generations (increased divorces woman emancipation), so their lifestyles and consumption habits are formed in a dissimilar manner than they used to. They are considered to be an autonomous skeptical group of consumers. Generation Y (born 1994 and after) are considered to be idealistic and optimistic. Both X and Y generation members grew up with a TV and lived Internet and personal technologies from the very beginning. Therefore, they consume products and services differently from previous and next generations (Yamamoto, 2010).

The *Millennial Generation* is the one which hasn't spent a part of their life without computer. Their philosophy is that the younger you are, the more information you can obtain and—as no surprise—this information is attained with a single click. They are impatient, flexible, and curious on exploring new areas and are value-oriented. These consumers (aged between 15 and 25) are able to use more than one medium simultaneously (Yamamoto, 2010).

The *Cell Generation* is not yet included to the labor force, but marketers should take into account that when they are included to the labor force this generation will appear with an aging population (Yamamoto, 2010).

Generation V can be considered a group that prefers online activities rather than actual physical experiences. The traditional demographics (age, sex, location) are not sufficient for marketing segmentation. They should be evaluated by online or mobile activities. This generation creates online characters, so marketers should aim to the character adopted or created and not to the person itself (Yamamoto, 2010).

Even though different generations adopt different opinions and behaviors, new generations are influenced by previous ones. Businesses in order to be successful should be able to maintain equal distances from each generation. The new generation is pursuing success, the best of everything, and they want things fast and easily.

Generation Y is seeking many options, adopting products or services according to their needs, and trying before buying. *Generation X* seems to be more passive and less active. For the marketers the challenge is that young age customers need to be treated especially according to their personality and not massively. This statement should become the new norm (Yamamoto, 2010).

The examination of these characteristics is only a rough approach of understanding the mobile consumer. They provide the first valuable differences and underline the need for a better and deeper examination of the mobile consumer. They are the first warning messages to marketers in their attempt to communicate with their potential consumers.

But who is the mobile consumer and how do consumers use their mobile devices around the world? The answer is coming in the next paragraphs, presenting facts from various surveys around the world.

The Mobile Consumer

It is certain that around the world consumers adopt different habits. Both high-growth and developed economies consumers in their vast majority own a mobile phone. Whether it is a smartphone or a feature phone, one would assume that developed markets would demonstrate higher smartphone ownership compared to high-growth markets. This assumption is not always true as, for example, when comparing South Korea (67% smartphone ownership) with US (61%). South Koreans also are the champions of mobile phone ownership (99%) while the UK and the US ownerships reach 97% and 94%, respectively. As for the demographics men tend to own smartphones more often than women and young consumers more frequently than older ones. The general trend is that smartphone purchases will augment as young consumers age. Also some consumers own more than one phone device (Russians 51% and Brazilians 48%) (Nielsen Research, 2013).

The selection criterion for the purchase of a mobile device varies. Chinese consumers are more interested in an easy-to-use device (31%), while the US consumers seek value for money (30%). Good operating system is important for Brazilians (24%), and stylish design for Russians (23%) (Nielsen Research, 2013).

Android devices have significantly increased their lead in overall popularity, with 71% reporting that Android is their primary mobile device of choice (versus 55% in 2013), while iOS devices were reported at 18% (versus 31% in 2013). The young report Android smartphones as their primary device, from 59% in 2013 to 67% in 2014. In terms of mobile phones, 61% of those surveyed said that Android phones are their primary device, with 17% reporting iPhones as their primary device. In addition, 64% of Europeans reported using Android phones, with only 13% using iPhones (Adobe, 2014).

Smartphones vs. Tablets

Smartphones continue to be the primary device over tablets (84%). However, participants state that they spend more time daily on their tablets now as compared to 2013. Of the middle-age segment, 39% reported spending 1 to 4 hours daily on their tablets (compared to 26% in 2013), followed by the older segment at 38% (versus 28% in 2013) and the young segment at 32% (versus 26% in 2013). Respondents overwhelmingly use their tablets at home, rather than at work or out and about (Adobe, 2014).

The most common activities the young engage with on tablet remain the e-mail communication, playing games, and viewing videos. Furthermore, there is an increase in shopping in the segment of young, from 43% in 2013 to 52% in 2014 (Adobe, 2014).

Mobile Activities

As for the mobile activities, text messaging is the most popular, followed by others like multimedia activities, Internet banking, and social media (average number of sent messages in the US is 764). Russians use their mobiles mostly for text messaging (95%), Brazilians for social networking (75%), and South Korean and Chinese use them for mobile shopping (43%). Applications increase in popularity, especially regarding games and social networking.

The audience for media on mobile is extremely huge. The top activities that consumers engage in are social media (58%), accessing local content (41%), and playing games (40%). Depending on the activity, consumers prefer either applications for social media (59%), games (58%), and music (57%) or mobile websites for magazines (60%), sports (65%), and news (65%) (Adobe, 2014).

Another potential of a mobile phone is watching videos, even though their screen is rather small. Mobile owners watch videos via mobile web or applications in most cases. Among mobile users, the ones in developed countries watch less often videos on their device compared to developing countries. The US users are the exception to the rule: 31% responded positive to video watching several times a day (Nielsen Research, 2013). Traditional TV viewing seems to be an irreplaceable habit. Only in South Korea consumers stated that they reduced TV watching (21%), while

15% declared they augmented traditional TV viewing. The majority of mobile device owners is still consuming the same or even more time on TV watching as they used to, even though now they have the mobile alternative (Nielsen Research, 2013).

In order to create value, marketers are targeting their audience with the right vehicle. In the developed world smartphone owners will probably receive an advertisement via applications: in Russia (34%) through text messaging and in China (32%) from video games or location-based services. Mobile owners receive an ad on their phone, in most cases once a day. How about the feelings of the consumers receiving an ad on their devices? Indian consumers are the most tolerant on receiving ads, yet they are less likely to receive one compared to other countries. UK (14%) and Australians (13%) are less likely to give personal information in order to receive customized ad content, while Indians (52%) favor ads that incorporate multimedia elements compared to simple text ads (Nielsen Research, 2013).

Moreover, comScore survey (2013) examined the impact of connected devices on consumer behavior. Summary of the findings are presented here.

Android and iOS dominate the US and EU

Multidevice/multiplatform is the new normal

High-speed, ubiquitous connectivity has unleashed mobile content consumption

Application usage dominates mobile web

Mobile is changing the way of shopping

Smartphone penetration in the EU: 57% in the EU on average, Germany 51%, Italy–France 53%, the UK 64%, Spain 66%

New devices bought: 8 in 10 are smartphones

Android and iPhone account for nearly 90% of the US smartphones

Android OS has the largest market share (53.4%), followed by Apple (36%)

iPad owners in their majority (60%) use an iPhone

Mobile accounts for 37% of time spent online in the US

Number of mobile video audience increases significantly faster than forPC

Applications dominate time spent for entertainment (90%), social media (90%), games (95%), technology (90%), business (80%) compared to the web

US smartphone owners frequently use their devices to make a purchase: 14% daily, 31% once a week, 55% one to three times a month

52.4% of US smartphone owners use their phone for shopping activities while in a retail store:
- 42% took a picture of the product
- 35% called family or friends for a product
- 22% compared product prices
- 18% found coupons
- 10% checked product availability

Source: comScore (2013). The impact of connected devices on consumer behavior—a comparison of the US and European mobile consumer behavior

All these valuable insights provide a guide to marketers in their attempt to map the mobile consumer and its dynamic context.

SoLoMo Consumers Are Mobile

With a closer look at mobile consumers, a more vulnerable segment is recognized. These consumers connect frequently on multiple devices from multiple locations and use a variety of applications, profiles based on their attitudes and behaviors compared to the rest of the mobile audience. Adobe report (2014) called them as the mobile elite (ME).

Demographically, these consumer segment slightly skewed to the young and middle-aged ranges (34% and 36%, respectively, with 30% from the older age range) and toward males (53% male versus 47% female). Additionally, they reported a slightly higher number of mobile devices being used: 1.9 for the ME versus 1.8 for the general consumer (Adobe, 2014).

Purchasing products through mobile devices increase year by year. ME consumers reported that they accessed visual information frequently (47% versus 38% for general consumers), while product and price information was also accessed more frequently (65% versus 58% for general consumers). Moreover, they prefer mobile applications for shopping, than mobile websites and then regular websites. General consumers also prefer mobile applications for shopping, but they reported as second preference the regular websites. The key point is that consumers prefer mobile applications for shopping, and therefore, marketers have to adopt the appropriate mobile strategy that prioritizes applications (Adobe, 2014).

The ME reported the use of mobile wallet (22%), augmented reality (13%) and mobile assisted in-store shopping (36%) compared to general consumers (14%, 9% and 32%) respectively.

Nielsen mobile path report (2013) reveals the UK consumer's purchasing behavior and the use of mobile devices. Smartphone has been the best option for consumers to seek for the products they want because it is "always on" but is less popular for the whole duration of the process than the tablet (18% vs. 23%) (Nielsen Research, 2013). Although most of the consumers know what they are looking for when they start browsing, there are those who still have to make a decision during their searching in their mobiles. Mobiles are a means of searching for retail information such as tablet or smartphone, but over 30% of tablet users want to make a purchase within the hour, suggesting more determined users. Where consumers are at home, the tablet is chosen (88%) over the smartphone which is mostly used at school or during traveling (25%). Smartphones are mainly used for comparing prices (77%) and finding online deals (43%) and less for reading reviews. Over half of smartphone and tablet owners are satisfied with the information available with a slight edge to tablet users' percentage, resulting in 55% and 61% respectively. A fact to be kept in mind, though, is that further improvement is both possible and desired by them all. Last but not least, half of consumers want business locations under search to be within 5 miles or closer at most from their location, with roughly 25% of them including a physical visit in their research (Nielsen Research, 2013).

Those results indicate that the ME are the consumers who take greater advantage for emerging mobile tactics, and therefore, it is more likely to be influenced by advertising and promotional tactics. It is certain that SoLoMo consumer is among this ME (Adobe, 2014).

The point is that SoLoMo consumers interact with businesses from multiple devices—and even cross-channel, such as starting from Facebook to a mobile site or application and then offline in a store or physical location. SoLoMo consumers are active mobile users, using mobiles to aid in their physical shopping experiences, from researching and comparing products to looking up customer reviews to locating specific products within a brick-and-mortar store.

The marketers have to recognize and understand the complexity of the consumer's journeys in which they are "lost" in order to optimize their mobile experience and to consider mobile as a vital platform in a true cross-channel approach to customer communications and engagement (Adobe, 2014).

Multiscreen and Multitask Behavior

Nowadays, consumers use a variety of devices to connect to one another and to their favorite content. In these devices are included the PC/laptop, smartphone, tablet, connected TVs, and games consoles.

The challenge for manufacturers and retailers who try to reach the consumers who are always connected is to think of the complex way in which consumers use multiple devices for different purposes. This dynamic is changing greatly by market and segment and also by the devices and content that are introduced for making consumers' lives easier.

In 2014, IpsosMediaCT investigated the "connected consumer" and the different screen behavior. In this survey they used more than 16,000 online interviews across 20 markets. The frame was from two groups of countries: Brazil, Russia, India, and China (BRIC), and UK. The findings provide a speculation context where the traditional marketing thinking and ways of approaching the potential consumer are in doubt.

The Connected Consumer

Thirty-three percent of online consumers in BRIC countries are in "least-connected group," whereas in the UK only 25% of the consumers are in this group. Furthermore, in BRIC and the UK the adoption rate of connected TVs is higher, while in Western Europe smartphone and tablet usage is higher.

Both in BRIC countries and the UK, smartphone usage is personal and is closely linked to social networking, e-mailing, messaging, and web browsing, whereas a connected TV is a shared screen and is used for "collective viewing" of broadcast events, movies, music, and multiplayer games. However, the tablet usage is for both personal and shared activity (IpsosMediaCT, 2014).

Communication

Over recent years traditional SMS messaging is still widely used by the UK consumers (83%), whereas it is used only by43% of online consumers in Asia. Moreover, it seems that the 78% of UK consumers are making traditional voice calls via their smartphone, while in Japan there is a much higher prevalence of mobile-based e-mail for this type of communication.

In recent years it seems that the use of images and video in messages has increased. So, around 33% of consumers in Asia and BRIC countries are picture messaging via a smartphone, but the UK falls behind. Also, picture/video messaging via a tablet is actually much lower in the UK (16%) than in BRIC countries (38%), which suggests a much more "family-based" use of messaging services in the UK.

The 17% of online consumers in BRIC markets use the VoIP apps via a smartphone (most noticeably in China—26%), while only 10% of online consumers in the UK use these apps. Interestingly, the use of VoIP apps on a tablet is higher both in the UK (18%) and in BRIC countries (35%) (IpsosMediaCT, 2014).

Entertainment: TV, Music, Gaming

It appears that online consumers mostly use their tablets, and not their smartphones, to watch TV. In more detail, in UK mostly the tablet owners (47%) in comparison with smartphone owners (11%) are using their devices to watch TV. On the other hand, in BRIC countries, the 19% of smartphone owners and 70% of tablet owners are using their devices to do so (IpsosMediaCT, 2014).

These marked differences are due to historical patterns of BRIC markets having skipped fixed broadband and moved straight to mobile connection. Media planners need to be mindful of these market differences as this may present significant opportunities for brands to capture a consumer's attention and click through to optimized content for that device.

It appears that online consumers in BRIC countries use their mobile and tablet devices more to listen to music than consumers in the UK. According to the survey, 36% of smartphone owners and 33% of tablet owners in the UK use their devices to listen to music. In the BRIC countries, due to a younger demographic population, 55% use their smartphone and 41% use their tablet (IpsosMediaCT, 2014).

The UK consumers use their smartphone less for gaming (33%) compared to the other consumers and especially to consumers in India who use their mobile to do so (47%). That may be because in India mobile gaming is dominated by "free to play" or "advertising models" and currently very limited in-app purchase. However, gaming on a tablet is highest overall in the UK (57%), and with global sales of tablets projected to outperform PCs in 2015, mobile gaming is seen as a growing trend in expanding markets like Asia and particularly Japan.

Moreover, Millward Brown's (2014) "AdReaction—Marketing in a multiscreen world" survey disclosed very interesting results showing the change behavior in the digital multiscreen era. This global survey was conducted with more than 12,000 multiscreen users, aged 16 to 45, across 30 countries. We present the major findings indicating the shift on the consumer's behavior:

- The global multiscreen user consumes almost 7 hours of screen media daily!
- The global multiscreen user spends most of his or her time with the smartphone screen (35% of the total screen media time within a day).
- Smartphones are the largest single screen medium around the world.
- Both smartphone and tablet usage represent an almost half the daily time (47% of all screen time).
- Watching TV and connected to Internet via laptop represent 27% and 26%, respectively, of the total screen media daily time.
- Among the 30 countries, findings revealed differences in overall screen minutes: generally, smartphone dominates the screen minutes except in the UK, France, and Spain where the TV watching has the first role.

- The global multiscreen user spends 30% of overall screen daily time watching TV and using a digital screen simultaneously: half of this time he or she does something on the Internet which is related to what he or she watches.
- The global multiscreen user most of the time combines using smartphone and watching TV, followed by using of laptop and watching TV; last is the tablet using–TV watching couple. It is certain that laptops and smartphones can be characterized as partners for the majority of people.
- Watching TV and being online via smartphone is the two most popular starting points of multiscreen behavior.
- TV advertising remains as the ad type with the most positive attitude and attracts more attention when comparing with the other digital mediums. On the other hand, ads delivered via a digital context—mostly by smartphones and tablets—have more potential to create purchase intention!
- The smartphone is a "do it all" device, providing opportunities to the user to engage in social media, searching info and related content to watch or discuss, and generally it represents an Internet "excavator" (only for US consumers).
- Laptop is a "productivity tool" for thorough searching content and for "demanding" tasks (only for US consumers).
- Tablet could be seen as an "entertainment" mean, alternative to TV (only for US consumers).

(Millward Brown, 2014)

Do you want more evidence of the new multiscreen behavior era? Another set of interesting findings comes from IAB Australia (2013) Multi-Screen Research confirming that the game has shift field from single to multiscreen behavior. These facts and numbers are challenging marketers to be responsive to the new multiscreen era and to make the appropriate adaptation on marketing strategies:

- 75% of the respondents adopt a multiscreen behavior.
- Share of screen attention:
  - 60% of people often use a second screen while using the TV screen.
  - 35% of people infrequently use a second screen while using the TV screen.
  - 5% of people never use a second screen.
- Attention is fragmented across all screens.
- TV sharing
  - TV + smartphone 30%
  - TV + laptop 33%
  - TV + PC 19%
  - TV + tablet 31%
- People listen to the TV screen. The "new radio"!
- Multiscreen use is the highest while the TV screen is on: multiscreen is TV + another screen.
- Women involve in multiscreen use while the TV is on: they are more social, and phones/laptops facilitate sharing.
- The **Fear Of Not Knowing (FONK)** is the new **Fear Of Missing Out (FOMO)**: it is not knowing that matters, it is all about being in the know.
- TV means content: people watch TV across all of their screens.
- People interact more with ads seen on laptops/desktops than on phones: it is a more active device.
- Ads in digital environments are seen as annoying interruptions: but most people do click through.
- Digitalization clearly drives sales: from awareness and advocacy to attitude change and action.

(IAB Australia, 2013)

All these important facts underline the need of shifting the focus from a static consideration of the consumer's behavior to a more holistic approach incorporating the mobile era and multiscreen behavior and their consequences. TV ads are not enough to capture consumer attention and have to be placed also in complimentary screens; smartphone confirms the impact of TV and whatever second screen strategy should be the first line of approaching the youth and the SoLoMo consumer. Traditional marketing activities and tools seem not to be enough to attract the consumer in this new context. Marketers have to take into account the multiscreen and multitask consumer behavior if they want to develop a competitive offer. Mobile marketing strategy is a crucial part of an integrated strategy aiming to target to the prospect consumer delivering an appropriate experience. In the next paragraph we will go through the major elements of a mobile strategy.

Mobile Marketing Strategy

The mobile era has created a new context in the marketing strategy formulation and implementation. There is an urgent need for rethinking the old rules and axioms. The aim is to compose a bundle of marketing activities using traditional and digital media. Mobile marketing strategy follows and supports "the big picture strategy" (Adobe, 2014).

It is apparent mobile devices have become the extension of our lives, an "alter ego," in such a way that marketers have to adapt their marketing strategy in the mobile era in order to provide a competitive offer with differentiation advantage. Mobile devices have an amazing characteristic: personalization! Marketers can capitalize on this and offer a customized experience to their consumers at a time and location they have chosen. This ability alone is not enough. Marketers have to understand consumers' mobile behavior and to provide them with the appropriate web services and mobile applications, making their shopping trip comfortable and supportive. As we have discussed in previous chapters, the dynamic technology environment has created a new web reality with four dimensions: personal, social, local, and mobile.

Social media is too important to be left in choice. Social media are everywhere anytime, and taking into account that traditional advertising and communication media lose the ground of the consumer's trust, it is obvious they increase marketing value. The World Wide Web has knocked down the walls of time and place: news, comments, sales promotions, sales calls, reviews, activities, situations, even moods are transferred digitally everywhere upon our request or not. Our 24/7 companion, the mobile device provides this cyber world in a personalized manner and makes our experience more unique.

Mobile devices such as smartphones and tablets are responsible for the dust on the PC. The access to web through mobiles is transcending our "best friend" at home or work, the personal computer/desktop. This is true, and the only thing you have to do is to go back to the previous paragraphs and see the facts from the surveys. Moreover, as you came across Chapter 3, nowadays consumer is acting in a more local manner. It is not enough for marketers to provide accurate content at a time that consumer wants but also apparent to offer a local context and competitive proposition.

All these dimensions of the new web reality lead to the "era of engagement" (Adobe, 2014). In this new era, marketer confronts a blear situation when mapping consumer online and offline behavior, and the challenge is becoming more adventuresome.

Yesterday's thoughts and experimental attempts are today's axiom. The current target audience—the consumer—seeks for a marketing offer which will give them a similar personalized experience regardless the place and the time they are: on the web in general, on Facebook, or in store. The challenge for the businesses and marketers is to incorporate all these elements and factors affecting consumer behavior into a mobile marketing strategy, adopting the appropriate effective tools.

But which of these marketing tools will provide an attractive experience to the loyal as well as the prospect consumer? Before the disclosure of the necessary attributes of a mobile marketing strategy it is crucial to discuss some "rule of thumb" floating in the marketplace.

The mobile applications are not a panacea. Applications probably attract a proportion of the potential consumers and may work better with the loyal consumers, but this is not the "only" issue. Evidence from global surveys suggests that the majority of the potential consumers prefer to use the web page of the retailer or manufacturer (Ericson et al., 2014) than to download and install their applications. Marketers first have to develop a friendly mobile web page, and then their applications could provide supportive elements and features to the consumer with caution: whatever the features provided, they have to be valuable to the consumer; an application for the application is without sense.

Moreover there is a lot of noise about some "trendy" mobile sites. An overloaded mobile site does not necessarily lead to marketing effectiveness. Again, findings indicate that consumers want simplicity and efficacy: easy checkout, a handy way of putting their preferences into their basket or dropping them, and of course a suitable-for-mobile site navigation (Ericson et al., 2014). These three features are not new ones but till nowadays are the major causes for the consumers to leave a site.

Another serious concern in the marketplace is the "showrooming" effect. The consumer visits a store to see the product, and maybe he or she will purchase it from another bricks-and-mortar store or online shop. This is not a myth, since almost half of the consumers use their smartphones in a physical store and most of them absolutely compare the prices (Ericson et al., 2014). But this is one side of the moon. At the same time that consumers compare prices when they are in a store; they also prefer in-store customer service and convenient. Further the in-store customer service has been more demanding: consumer has made a thorough search, compared prices and product attributes, and put the step in the store to find the expert floor sales people providing a personalized experience (Ericson et al., 2014). Moreover probably he or she wants to communicate with a mobile sales assistant in order to feel that the store is the right one for his or her needs.

The secret behind these concerns is a responsive mobile website reflecting features and characteristics that any consumer wants. A mobile website will be a part of an integrated digital communication strategy delivering a coherent content to all various channels: website, social media, mobile applications...an omnichannel marketing strategy.

Mobile marketing strategy has to be structured on the understanding of consumer shopping journey. In the next lines the major dimensions of this fascinating journey are presented:

- Look at the data: size and composition of your mobile audience; types of mobile devices they use and relative operating systems; the ways of using their mobile devices;

how they search and where they search; which social media they use; what kind of check-in behavior they have; the degree of accepting promos, coupons, and ads; the payment methods they prefer; the usage rate of QR codes.

- The content and the services to be delivered to the consumer must be personal and consistent across channels. Meaningful targeting is also desirable: the right message to the right audience.

- Adaptation, adaptation, adaptation: Begin with developing a mobile website appropriate for different types of devices. One single platform incorporating properties and applications that operate under various mobile devices could solve many future operational and technical obstacles.

- Keep it simple: a mobile-friendly interface offering simplicity in navigating, searching, and browsing.

- Listen to the consumer: feedback is as important as the right message to the right audience. Mobile means communication and in turn means ways of getting the feedback from the consumer and responding in real time with accuracy.

- Communicate consistent content across all channels attempting to create conversations.

- Integration: mobile marketing strategy is a part of the "big strategy." The isolated marketing activities are only waste of time and money (scarce resources).

If you want to acquire loyal consumers, first you must understand their behavior and needs and then translate them into a targeted mobile user personal experience. Analyzing the consumer's physical and digital behavior is the key for the marketers to provide a competitive experience and hopefully giving an advantage to their offer.

The winners in the new Social, Local, and Mobile marketing era will be those who develop a thorough understanding of the shopping decision journey that consumers undertake and what really matters when it comes to shopping.

CHAPTER 5

SoLoMo Tools and Applications

In this chapter you will read:

- What the mobile web is
- About the latest digital marketing tools
- Which social media tools to use
- Which local marketing tools work
- Which mobile marketing tools respond better to the SoLoMo strategy
- About the next-generation SoLoMo applications
- An explanation of the I.N.T.E.R.A.C.T. methodology
- The future implications for marketers

The Mobile Web

The mobile web is the natural extension of the development of the Internet, from the first hypertext pages through "Web 2.0" and onto social. In order to understand what the mobile web offers businesses in terms of marketing, it is worthwhile reflecting on the development of online resources and how they have each shaped and changed the way brands engage their customers.

When the Internet was first developed it was little more than a series of static pages linked together through hypertext links, the so-called World Wide Web. The users did not have any interaction with these websites; they could simply read what was on them and click on links to other pages. When the telecommunications infrastructure allowed higher bandwidths and computers could process more data, the age of "Web 2.0" was born. This simply meant that sites became much more complex, because the technology was there to run them feasibly. This created one major change; rather than simply reading what was on a site, users could now interact with it; they could post up things like text, video, photos, and other such materials.

This meant that sites such as YouTube, MySpace, Bebo, Flickr, Facebook, and LinkedIn became possible, because they rely on user-generated content. What is more, they allowed people to put up content and share it directly with people they know, through networks of friends on sites such as Facebook. As this developed over time, it became a key advertising space as it allowed adverts to be targeted very specifically around users' personal interests, tastes, and browsing habits, much more effective than mass marketing (Evans, 2012).

What is absolutely critical about this shift is that it fundamentally altered the dynamic of information flow between brands and customers. Formerly, brands simply broadcast information to customers through mass marketing campaigns, and there was little possibility of sustained customer feedback or engagement. Social media changed this completely; for the first time customers could give feedback en masse; websites like TripAdvisor revolutionized the hotel industry because it allowed for the aggregation of customer feedback totally outside the control of the hotel owners. More recently, companies that are perceived to have done something wrong can be the victim of a "Twitter Storm" whereby they receive so much comment on the site that it shows up in trending metrics and is all visible to the general public.

Thus, brands have had to become much more responsive in the way they engage with their customer. They now no longer simply talk with them, but seek to build a positive relationship with them based on interactive communications; many businesses now handle customer service enquiries through Twitter because that is their customers' preferred method of contact. Brands also have to be much more responsive—and careful—about how they deal with customer complaints, because social media means that many of these exchanges now take place in full view of the public, or could very easily end up there (Tuten and Solomon, 2014).

At the same time the web was becoming more social and interactive, the process of technological convergence was changing the devices that were used to access the Internet. Cell phones and PDAs became progressively more complex and able to access the Internet, and then there was the advent of the smartphone. The smartphone combined many of the features found on other devices with an impressive level of computing power to make them, in effect, miniature computers. Smartphones enable high-quality Internet browsing, e-mails, high-quality photographs, play music, play games, and work with an ecosystem of applications that allow the user to do all kinds of things from booking flights to searching for restaurant recommendations.

In the context of this book, there are two key features of the smartphone that are particularly relevant. The first is that they all have a GPS transponder in them, and so can be geolocated with a very high degree of accuracy. The second is that the ecosystem of applications play host to many social networks, particularly Facebook and Twitter. These social networks work well with smartphones because they allow people to create and share content in real time; rather than waiting until they get home to use a computer. The fact that they can take photographs and videos enhances this.

The combination of social apps, local targeting, and mobile devices has given rise to the acronym SoLoMo or Social, Local, Mobile. These are the three pillars of a contemporary mobile marketing campaign, and there are a multitude of ways that people are using the ability to target people based on where they are and the social apps that they use. A good example would be the placement of advertisements for restaurants on the Facebook app based on location, time of day, and recent social activity suggesting the user wants to go out that evening.

There are further examples where companies are using local devices to connect to the smartphones of the shopper as they are walking past the store or they are browsing the shelves. These devices, for example, the iBeacon, connect via Bluetooth or the in-store Wi-Fi network if the user has connected to that, and directly puts adverts on the screen of the smartphone, by means of the messaging service on the phone. This allows them to alert shoppers to special offers, similar products, encourage them to leave feedback, and otherwise make a purchase.

Digital Marketing Tools

Social Tools

Foursquare is a simple tool that lets people "check in" when they reach a particular location such as a restaurant, coffee shop, or bar. Business owners can register their individual businesses on the site, and then provide a selection of special offers for people who check in with them. Usually these offers are tied in with other social actions, such that they become active when people share their check-in on other social media.

Foursquare business—Foursquare is a program that encourages consumers to "check in" and let their social networks know where they are and what they are doing. As a business you can register your location and provide offers that will provide incentives for your customers to take some kind of action, including sharing with their network.

TripAdvisor—for any business in the hospitality, travel or leisure business, or really anybody with physical premises that customers visit, TripAdvisor is essential. The site allows people to leave feedback about venues that they have visited; venue owners can register and then respond to customer feedback. The site is very large in its own right, but TripAdvisor ratings are used on many other sites as a de-facto measure of quality, and so engaging with the site is crucial.

Twitter—a lot of companies use Twitter as a de-facto customer service experience, because it is very easy for people to ask short questions directly to the brand and for the brand to reply to them in as equally as quickly. Twitter also offers a level of engagement with people, as brands often "retweet" things that people have shared with them when having a positive experience with their company.

Facebook pages—these are becoming increasingly important for companies because they draw together many of the features of other social media sites. It is possible to check in as you would on Foursquare, users can rate the brand out of five stars as you might on TripAdvisor, and the company can interact very simply with customers through their "wall" quite like they would on Twitter. Facebook also has by far and away the largest number of users as well, and is important for that reason alone.

Local Tools

Blogging might not seem like a location-specific tool because they can be read by anybody anywhere. In a technical sense that is true, but the content of the blog tends to dictate the readership in the main. In that sense blogs that are built entirely around a location can be very powerful SoLoMo marketing tools.

A good example of this would be a blog that reviews New York food outlets. While the blog could be read by anybody in the world, the bulk of its readership will come from the New York area. Moreover, the blog can be targeted at particular types of eatery such that this further delineates the audience for the blog. Securing a review or placement on such a location-specific blog can be an extremely powerful take for generating a local following.

Coupon Apps

There are a lot of coupon apps out there. Perhaps the most well-known is Groupon, which allows companies to create special offers for a small fee, which should drive customers to particular outlets. For example, an ice cream store might offer a coupon for a free extra scoop at its Boston branches on the following Saturday. The consumer logs on to Groupon and gets the coupon on their phone, and hopefully shares it with their friends via social media as well. The advantage to the local business is that it is easy to set up, as Groupon provides the infrastructure, and is a fast way of generating local interest. There are aggregators such as The Coupons App which is a free download for consumers to get coupons from multiple different providers, such as local free coupon sites. There are also extensions for WordPress websites that allow small business to offer coupons directly through their own sites for as little as $10 a month. There are services such as Grocery IQ which is the same essential design but focused around a very specific market segment, with some added functionality to suit those industries such as creating copping lists and matching coupons to items on the list.

Mobile Tools

As mentioned in previous chapters, ensuring websites are responsive to mobile devices is crucial in delivering a SoLoMo campaign. There are a number of tools that will help you understand whether your website is mobile friendly and how to improve its optimization. You need to be extremely thorough in this process, because you need to track your entire customer journey through from start to finish and do so using all the different types of mobile browser that are out there; they all have subtle differences and you need to be on top of them all. A sloppy customer experience on the mobile site will result in an enormous drop-off rate through the customer journey, so it is essential to get it right. A good service is the phone emulator Mobile Moxie, which is a free tool that lets you see how your website will look when displayed on various mobile devices; as it is a free tool the selection of browsers and devices to emulate is limited, but it is a very good start.

For those with relatively limited technical skills there are a number of services that can provide an automatic conversion of your current website to a mobile version, though inevitably this is not quite as polished as designing the site from the ground up with mobile in mind.

Duda Mobile offers free and premium wizards to convert your site to mobile site in a straightforward step-by-step process. Bmobilized is a slightly different option, because you can either follow their step-by-step wizard yourself or simply pay them a one-off fee and they will do the conversion for you. Mobify is a better solution for large websites and enterprise-level solutions, as it has a much more complex level of functionality compared to the former two. When using these tools it is important to use tools like Google analytics to understand how customers have been finding your site in the past, and use the redesign for mobile as a jumping off point for improving that.

Apps

As previous chapters argued, apps are incredibly important, and are not all that expensive to procure from scratch. However, some people may not have the technical knowledge to be able to specify a new application from scratch even if it is just to instruct an app designer on what they are looking for. With that in mind there are a number of free apps and tools available to smooth the process. If you are in a B2B sector, then LinkedIn is a very useful tool for finding and engaging with leads or prospective customers with very little effort. The app is intuitive and has a large subscriber base, meaning it is easy to find and add people whom you meet in real life.

Next-Generation SoLoMo Apps

Venture capital money has been pouring into SoLoMo apps (indeed, it was a VC executive that coined the acronym), and there are set to be a plethora of new services aiming to remake the social, local, and mobile landscape, which underlines the importance of always having one eye on the future. SoLoMo is defined by an incredibly fast pace of change and development, so it is not enough to simply understand and master the apps that are relevant at the moment.

SoLoMo Applications

GetGlue

Allows people to check in as watching particular TV shows or films as you might a physical location, with a view to building a shared community around those things. Serves recommendations based on check-ins.

Trover

Shares discoveries from within locations rather than indicating presence at a location; so, for example, it might be sharing photos of things within a historical site rather than just checking in there.

myShopanion

Aims to socialize the shopping experience for normal products by creating a conversation around them. Browsers can ask questions, seek opinions, and chat about particular products, and they can accomplish various tasks like actually buying the product, or adding it to a wish list.

ShopSavvy

Allows users to compare and research products as they physically stand in the store. The app uses bar code scanning technology through the camera function to determine what the product is, offering online research, reviews, and alternative outlets. This is combined with GPS tracking that shows the nearest alternative outlets.

ThinkNear

Allows stores to offer flash-sale type short-term offers to customers who are geographically proximate to the store. This can help smooth out slow periods and introduce new customers to the store.

Stampt

This is similar to ShopSavvy in that it uses phone functionality to scan products which then add up to a loyalty bonus within that particular store, so it is essentially a digital loyalty card. Moreover purchases are placed in a CRM system so that the retailer can follow up with targeted offers based on previous purchases.

I.N.T.E.R.A.C.T.

The I.N.T.E.R.A.C.T acronym is short for the following areas of discussion and should frame everything that goes into a SoLoMo strategy.

- Integration.
  All of the proprietary and third-party elements of social media campaign, such as the mobile website and Facebook page, should be seamlessly integrated to present an excellent customer experience.
- Notification.
  Brands should not be passive. They should be using social media notification settings to actively deliver offers and information.
- Traffic.
  Volume is the lifeblood of any online enterprise, so everything that the company says or does in public should be geared around generating more traffic.

- Education.
  Social media is an excellent opportunity to educate consumers
  about products and services, how they can make the most of
  them, and how they can be upsold.
- Relationships.
  Social media is not just about the "transaction"; it is about
  building up the long-term engagement with a customer that
  keeps them coming back for more.
- Access.
  Social media knows no opening hours. It is a 24/7 endeavor.
- Community.
  Social media is a multichannel experience. Customers talk to each
  other about your brand, for better or for worse (Kamins, 2014).
- Transactions.
  The end goal of every element of social media marketing, howev-
  er indirect, is to convert sales (Motameni and Nordstrom, 2014).

Implications for Marketers

The SoLoMo phenomenon has completely changed the way that marketers have to operate their campaigns; from the way that they even
conceive of their relationship with the customer, through to the way
that they design and operate campaigns themselves. The crux of the
matter is that there has been a convergence in marketing as much as
there has been a convergence in technology.

There are many companies and consultants who will offer to help
with any one component of SoLoMo. There are myriad agencies offering
social marketing services, consultants for mobile site design, and individual items like the iBeacon for location-based targeting. However, the key to
the SoLoMo idea is that they all work together; you cannot do one or two
of the three. They are in many ways mutually constitutive; social works
because mobiles are portable, location works because it ties in with social
habits and so on. Therefore, there is no sense in working on all of these
things independently.

Therefore, the implication for marketers is that they need to build
their capacities around all three elements. This will fundamentally alter

the way that companies engage with their customers, and marketers need to be very focused in order to get the best out of the process. The following elements will be absolutely critical in any SoLoMo marketing strategy:

- Engaging customers through geotriggered ads
- Linking as many parts of the customer experience as possible to the capabilities of the smartphone; using barcode scanning, photo-shopping, instant feedback and recommendation tools, and so on
- Creating instant rewards and incentives delivered through the mobile platform to create and maintain engagement
- Being proactive in dealing with multiple strands of live feedback through social and mobile sources, both positive and negative feedback
- Maintaining brand recognition and brand values in such a dynamic space

These are quite different competencies from digital marketers are used to, because they are not confined to any one channel or tool, or style of marketing, but represent marketing around the behaviors of customers. This will make it challenging to maintain a robust marketing campaign across all the methods of engagement and advertising that are in the SoLoMo world, so planning will be absolutely essential for any marketing team.

The SoLoMo world is also extremely fast paced. The sections above note that there are myriad new apps being developed with venture capital money, and any one of them could forge radical change in any given market space. On top of this, smartphone manufacturers are constantly battling to introduce new technologies into their devices such as retinal scanning and heartbeat monitors, which can all be inveigled into new SoLoMo means of engaging customers. Because of this, marketers always need to have one eye on the horizon; it will never be the case that marketers have got every SoLoMo base covered. They will always need to be aware of the latest developing trends and understand how that will impact upon what they are already doing.

CHAPTER 6

Where Is It All Going?

In this chapter you will read about:

- The new SoLoMo environment
- The NFC (near field communication) technology
- Wearable items
- New technologies
- Online brand reputation management
- Social media enterprises

Introduction

Over the last years the amount of change that we have witnessed as consumers is astounding. Some of the new technologies have managed to change the market place and revolutionize multiple industries in a very short period of time. Mobile phones are playing a huge role in this change. So far phones had to contact with cell towers in order to be able to be used. But a new era is rising! Now they can communicate with *our product and service retailers and new wearable technologies like the high-tech bangles on our wrists. The new technology is creating a totally new truly intelligent ecosystem.*

But what is the role of the business in this new environment where the technology is moving so fast that many firms are not able to keep up? These firms should aim to know and understand the customer to such an extent that the product or service fits them and practically sells itself. In other words we need to move ahead from simply knowing the consumer to understanding their needs.

The new system that is arising is no doubt flooded with smart technology and massive amounts of data. These will give the power to business and enable marketers to capture an intelligence that far surpasses anything in the past. With the use of the new technologies the products will be able to sell themselves because in the minds of the consumers they are positioned as helpful and needed.

The New Environment

The business environment is constantly changing, and firms need to be prepared in order to take advantage of the new opportunities that are created in a new ecosystem that accelerates creativity, innovation, and of course focuses a lot on entrepreneurial spirit (Ankeny, 2013).

The new idea is not only creating applications that the user needs to give the input every time, but creating applications that will learn from experience (Chaney, 2015). In this way they will be able to improve with every single interaction and with no doubt they will be able to assist the consumer into making simple and more complex purchase decisions. Other cognitive computing, which involves self-learning systems that use data mining and other pattern recognition, will change the industry environment and the society habits and patterns.

One of the main issues that consumers are facing today is that they have in their disposal an infinite amount of information, but unfortunately they have limited time to access it. Most of the devices that we are using today are relying on humans in order to receive the initial information. That leads to today's problem, which is the limited time, attention, and accuracy of the consumers.

As Oh et al. (2014) argue, new types of innovation in the near future will help consumers to manage massive amounts of consumer data. Since more and more devices are being connected to the Internet, more and more information will be shared among the users. That will inevitably lead to sharing of knowledge and experience. Firms are already focusing toward such extensions where the sharing of the shopping experience holds a centered role and more consumer data are available for brands.

The new environment is also demanding new types of technologies like different kinds of wearables (Bruno, 2015). Until now most manufactures have been focusing on wearables that have to do with health and fitness technology, but as tech moves beyond the activity tracker and becomes fundamental to our daily health and fitness, those wearables have a new meaning.

The new environment is without question characterized with mobile development. More and more new features are being incorporated into smartphones. This trend will not slow down since the mobile market has not settled yet. Following this trend the location-based mobile commerce and the applications built within the mobile environment will change industries in the next coming years. One great example is iBeacon which is a location-aware transmitter at all of their US retail stores, essentially providing to the company the ability to pass on product information to the consumers and allowing them to check out very quickly through their iPhone. The phone is now changing to a personalized map that reveals all the type of information that the consumer is interesting in and hiding all the irrelevant that could distract their shopping attention.

At the same time the new environment could incorporate some technologies that could definitely change the traditional way of shopping and that will make firms to rethink their online and offline strategies. Again with the use of iBeacon the consumer may pause in front of a concert poster in the underground metro station and just by scanning the code in the poster the consumer could just buy the ticket with a single tap. In that case the poster is basically the advertisement but at the same time the point of sales (POS) and the only point of contact with the consumer. That poster is becoming an "all in one point" of interaction.

Of course in this turbulent environment consumers crave recognition of their individuality, even though they are pleading for respect of their private life. This antithetical approach is quite intriguing for the marketing managers. One way to solve this issue is the collaborative consumption. For example, with the wearable technology consumers share information and brands must understand that it is not in their hands but in the hands of societal, economic, and tech-driven factors, for this information to be shared. Consumers are engaging themselves into platforms where they becoming part of the business model. This new type of trend in the business environment has to do mostly with thinking a new way of how different types of services are managed and consumed. New types of technologies give the firms opportunity to create a market where people with same goals could be connected. Basically it is the idea of "prosumption" in which customers are the producers and the consumers at the same time.

Another aspect that could enhance the formation of the new business environment is that of collaborative purchasing through branded crowdfunding. The firm that made this model quite popular is Kickstarter where basically the consumers "put their money where their mouth is." What Kickstarter does is focusing on enabling new brands using technology. This type of collaborative purchasing is the next wave of digital opportunities for brands. Branded crowdfunding can also create stronger signals from intent to actual purchase.

The NFC (Near Field Communication) Technology

Before we start analyzing the benefits of NFC technology for the firms and also for the consumers, let us first define what NFC is. NFC is enabling through wireless technology, data to be exchanged between two devices that are very close to each other (Dutot, 2015). The technology is simple. It is a short-range, low-power wireless link evolved from radio-frequency identification (RFID) tech that can transfer small amounts of data between two devices held a few centimeters from each other. Consumers, simply by bringing two NFC-enabled devices very close together, start automatically a communication in between those two devices without having to open any other applications.

Basically NFC technology is able to identify the consumers, connect to their bank account and communicate these information to the retailer in order to make a payment (Pham and Ho, 2015). But what is the actual difference between NFC technology and any other previous pairing technologies? The answer is very simple! There is no pairing involved. Our mobile phone does not need to be connected with another device. The only thing the consumers need to do is to tap their phones on a contactless payment terminal in a shop, train station or coffee shop and through the NFC technology the bank account of the user is going to be identified. But it does not stop there. Personal preferences and shopping habits are being spotted, making the purchase experience faster and easier.

Consumers want to be able to communicate with the firms in the easiest possible way. They usually forget their passwords of their different accounts, and sometimes they do not even remember that they have an account in a specific firm. How many times have we tried to register in a specific website and get back a message saying "This email is already being used. If you forgot your password please click here." Firms need to realize that consumers are in need of secure but extremely easy ways of access when they are buying products online. They are in need of instant intuitive connectivity, zero configuration, and smart key access, and NFC technology could offer that.

Retailers could make use of NFC technology mainly through four categories of NFC applications. The first one is the "Touch & Go." In order for the consumers to make use of this application they need to put the device reader close to the access code. The access code could be in a poster in bus station. For example, a concert is being advertised in a poster. The consumer could easily buy the ticket just by bringing close to the poster. Another category of NFC application is the "Touch & Confirm." In this category is included any mobile payment that the consumer needs to confirm just by simply entering a password in order to accept the transaction. The third category is called "Touch & Connect." Under this category we have all the data transfer that could happen between two mobile devices. It is essentially a peer to peer data transfer. In other words consumers could exchange instantly music, images, etc. In today's complex environment, mobile phones equipped with NFC technology will enable consumers to exchange personal data extremely fast with no effort at all. Just by bringing two NFC-equipped devices close to each other consumers will effortlessly exchange and store personal data. The fourth category is called "Touch & Explore." Consumers are able to explore different services that are being offered by the same retailer without even typing the URL in their browser. In other words the retailers could help consumer to read information and search special offers, coupons, and discounts from smart posters or smart billboards.

Undoubtedly the greatest advantage is that an NFC-enabled phone is able to make an online payment with no effort from the part of the consumer. That means that the consumer is not actually putting the product in the basket of the online store and return later to make the actual buy. They proceed directly to the buy and that is giving them less time to change their mind!

NFC mobile contactless payments can be made at both attended POS locations (such as stores) and unattended locations (such as vending machines) that use the existing merchant payments infrastructure. To pay, the consumer simply brings the phone to within a few inches of a contactless payment-capable POS system and the transaction occurs. It is the exact same process.

Of course since NFC is a fairly new technology that is being introduced it comes along with many concerns and especially with concerns that have to do with security issues, since this new type of technology has access to the bank accounts of the consumers. In order to reassure the consumers NFC technology uses different type of security levels for different applications. For example, payment account information and payment transactions are highly secure. All financial and personal information is stored in a secured area in the NFC phone, commonly called the "secure element." In other words, the application and payment account information are encrypted and stored in a secure area in the phone. On the other hand, if NFC technology I used for "Touch & Explore" applications then they might have little to no security. The phone that uses NFC technology to communicate with the retailers' contactless payment system is quite similar to the contactless payment cards and devices that we are using today and consumer are becoming more and more familiar. The payment processes are the same processes used when the consumer pays with a traditional contactless or magnetic stripe credit or debit payment card.

Wearable Items

While marketers are still learning how to leverage location-based marketing, wearable tech is becoming more and more popular and is wining grounds extremely fast in today's marketplace (Bruno, 2015). More and more firms are launching new accessories that either work as stand-alone products or need to be connected to the smartphone of the consumer. Either way it is becoming a huge trend. In general wearable items are quite expensive breakthrough products that are using extremely sophisticated technology. Firms need to differentiate and retailers need to make use of this new trend. Before analyzing the benefits and how retailers could incorporate in their marketing strategies the wearable technology lets identify the new trends of the wearable market.

Wearable fitness technologies have gained the broadest acceptance among consumers. We witness the future of health and fitness technology as tech moved beyond the activity tracker and become fundamental to our daily health and fitness. Instead of simply tracking our activity, they are actually guiding us. The question that firms are facing now is if the consumers will continue to buy limited-function devices when their smartphones can deliver a lot of the same value. A category by its self is Google Glass (Park and Skoric, 2015). Although the product is not widely available to consumers, Google Glass has empowered the firm to test the market and change the initial product to an intelligent personal assistant that will power the next generation of wearable tech devices (Kinnunen et al., 2016).

Another new category that is picking up really fast is the smart watches. Wearable tech watches are often designed as smartphone extenders, allowing users to see messages and caller ID without taking out their phones and are the category where fashionistas are making their mark. In addition to that and while it is still in its infancy, wearable tech jewelry offers highly targeted functionality. A ring that could look as a normal ring and with NFC technology it will be able to unlock doors and mobile devices.

The constantly changing environment, especially of the wearable market, is pushing for changes in the social media platforms. The current platforms are not yet optimized to receive information from the wearable items. The main reason for that is because most of the social media are designed for interaction to take place on screen-based devices, which is not the case for most of the new wearable items. The new devices have limited screens and in some case they have not at all, which means that the social media platforms will have eventually to adapt in order to facilitate meaningful interactions on wearable tech.

Wearable items will be able though to communicate with social network platforms automatically. Of course the authorization from the users' side will be necessary. Once the user approves that, then the wearable devices will be able to identify under which situation they could publish an update automatically. For example, if a smart watch detects that you run

5 km and burned 500 calories in a specific location and the user has pre-approved the sharing of fitness information, then the smart watch will automatically share this information in a social media platform.

Another feature which is underused is the voice recognition. In the wearable items where the screen is extremely small or even there is no screen, the voice recognition is going to play a really important role. Due to this fact a new era of social media is going to arise and new social media platforms will be developed just for voice.

New Technologies

The ever-present technology will challenge marketers to develop a sensor that could read people's biological responses when purchasing and using products and services. Responding to a customer's context may no longer simply be about their location, but more about their emotional state!

This new types of wearable technologies are offering to the retailers an amazing opportunity to understand the consumers. Sensors and display technologies are being embedded into clothing and they could identify in real time the emotional state of the consumer. These sensors could understand the different types of mood and levels of stress simply by just displaying light or a different color in order to inform both the wearer and those that are connected with him or her. Consumers don't want to suppress their negative emotions but at the same time they do not want to shout them out loud. Weirdly enough they are waiting from other people to "sense" their mood! A person wants real-time feedback from another person. There is a new concept in the market were just by wearing a vest you could feel another person's heartbeat as a vibration, so you would basically subscribe to the other person's heart rate data and then feel it inside of your vest. In that way you can respond immediately to the others person reactions.

The new technology incorporated with the wearable items could help retailers to capture things like a heart rate and then try to interpret that in their benefit. For example, if consumers are really excited about a brand then their heart rate will increase. If retailers now the exact moment that this will take place they could reinforce that feeling with an extra offer for example, or they could suggest some cross-sales through the app.

If retailers could understand the consumer's normal emotional state and could see in real time when it is getting out of normal range then they could have an amazing opportunity to intervene with some sort of experience that the person might be receptive to. In other words they could provide some sort of real-time help or feedback in the moment. Retailers could use wearable technology in order to provide consumers with convenience marketing, making the life of the consumer as easy as possible. Let us imagine the following scenario. You are running late for a business meeting and the traffic is terrible according to your online update. You prenotify your colleagues that you're running late based on your distance from the meeting and you call a taxi through an app. At the same time your phone detects high levels of stress and plays your favorite music in order to relax you.

Of course according to the previous scenario the consumers have given full access to their personal information. Firms need to set aside the inevitable questions of personal data and privacy, but at the same time they need to make consumers feel comfortable to give their personal data on the spot (i.e., detect emotions). The amount of data that is being gathered from the wearable items could open a total new field for the consumer behavior analysis. No company is currently broadcasting its intention to sell the data generated from wearable items, but it is going to be a matter of time. The fact that firms have enormous amount of data it doesn't mean that they can make full use of it. They need to have specialized people in the marketing team to perform data analysis. With this new technology the amount of data is going to be enormous and firms need to be able to interpret it.

Undoubtedly, the natural extension of these devices is to become from wearable to implantable. In the next years we will move from glasses to lenses and from clothes that show our mood to e-ink tattoos that light up and express our feelings in the current situation.

Online Brand Reputation Management

Brand reputation is the customers' perception of a company. Online reputation management is the process of controlling what shows up when someone Googles the name of your firm. The aim of every firm should be to promote a positive content to the top of every search result and at the same time all the negative ones should be pushed aside.

Many firms do not realize that they need to concern about their online reputation. Sometimes they are just wondering why people say bad things about them online, even though they have done nothing wrong. Building a strong brand is an ongoing and extreme difficult process that takes a long time. All that effort could be wasted just in a few days or even hours if something goes wrong. Sometimes the damage is so big that there is no way back. That could happen especially if the negative comments appear in websites that are really high in search engines, so anyone doing a search on the company name will probably see them. Sometimes those negative comments are true and sometimes are not. Either way they threaten the firm's well-being.

No matter how small or big your business is, the consumers and prospects are going to talk about you. Especially in today's hyper connected world the consumers are going to tweet about an event that your firm hold, they will leave a comment in your Instagram account and even in your Facebook page and so on. Regular interactions on social networks are vital to any business success. There is no way for a firm to avoid this! The only thing that can be done is to constantly scan the Internet. Online brand reputation management is not just social media monitoring, or online public relations, but it is a philosophy. Once the firm embraces that philosophy, the impact on sales is going to be enormous.

The philosophy of online brand management lies into the optimization of the brand content online. In order for firms to protect and enhance their brand visibility in the electronic environment they need first to apply best practices in order to optimize their brand content. These best practices of digital communications include search engine optimization (SEO), public relations, human resources, and related electronic content that is publicly available on the web as well as social media: text, images, audio, and video. Of course even if a firm follows all the above strategies that does not mean necessarily that they are in control, but at least it gives a head start.

When it comes to online brand management, firms need to be proactive. They must have a proactive monitoring campaign that will provide them with useful information of their different audiences. Proactivity is the answer to the online management troubles. If consumers are talking about our products or services on social media, we must take action on the spot in order to minimize the potential dangers. In today's hyperconnected social world, if we just ignore the situation, it is not going to diffuse by itself. The risk of not responding to negative comments or conversations could be huge. A negative tweet or Facebook post that goes viral will do unimaginable damage to your brand's reputation. There are tons of cases of brands getting destroyed or permanently scarred by either not responding to complaints online or responding back in a negative tone.

A question that may come in our mind is why we should manage our online brand reputation. The answer is quite simple. If our brand reputation is bad, then the consumers would not like to be associated with us. Our online reputation could easily create a strong brand, but at the same time it could destroy our firm over a night. An extremely easy way for the retailers to see their online reputation is simply to search over the Internet what is being said about them. Positive comments indicate a healthy firm and negative problems suggest actions for change. Of course all these negative comments should not be taken lightly. If there is a consumer who takes time to write even negative comments means that they want to be in a relation with our firm. If they didn't care at all, they would not even spend time and effort to do that.

Social Media Enterprises

In the recent years we are witnessing the new era, in which the firms are focusing mainly on the online environment. In some cases they tend to focus only on the online environment, giving up completely the offline one. Some firms are concentrating not only on the world of Internet but more on the world of apps. Of course as we mentioned in previous chapters, just offering an app is not good enough for the SoLoMo consumer. As a firm, we need to use a collection of tools that are going to entice, engage, and track the customers. Creating a social enterprise is about being social for the greater good of the business, in order to increase the firms' productivity and to lead to greater innovation.

We have witnessed numerous cases in which firms were inadequate in terms of communicating effectively the goals and the mission of the company internally. The dissemination of valuable information could take a long period of time in order to reach all the departments. Here is where a social media platform benefits the firm. The ability of transferring rapidly to the targeted internal audience valuable information among specific employee groups is one of the main benefits.

Just a few years ago, skepticism abounded over the place of enterprise social media. The greatest benefit is that the feedback that a social enterprise is getting is instant. For example, if a franchise retailer is doing two days sales promotion, the enterprise could easily have hourly updates through social platforms instead of waiting until the end of the day for a phone call or an e-mail from the franchise store. If enterprises didn't have that immediate feedback they would continue to base their promotions on limited historical sales data. But in the above-mentioned scenario the social enterprise is maximizing the operational objective through improved effectiveness of a weekend sales campaign. In terms of actual implementation firms could use some of the shelf products like Yammer. Of course firms may need to modify it in order to ensure that employees are using the software in the most effective way. One of the main obstacles of adopting such software is the ongoing configuration and customization throughout the process in order to ensure that the software is meeting the need of the firms and is increasing the communication in between the departments.

The question now is how well these offerings serve the purposes of collaboration and business transparency. Deloitte's recent survey (2014) on corporate culture suggests executives and employees are of distinctly differing opinions. For example, in the survey of 1,000 workers and 300 executives at US companies, 45% of executives said social media has a positive impact on their workplace culture, while only 27% of employees agreed. To protect the corporate brand, most large corporations have implemented social media policies to ensure that employees communicate appropriately across all social software channels. While social networking's success among consumers is well-documented, enterprise social media tools are still struggling to gain a foothold in organizations because of the confusion over how to best apply the technology to business operations, and concerns that it could be a drain on worker productivity.

Closing Remarks

SoLoMo is not another marketing method. It is not even a breakthrough, contemporary marketing strategy. One can claim that today's companies are actually using social media, local content, and mobile applications in their marketing plans. So what's the fuss about SoLoMo? We see SoLoMo as an approach to embrace new technologies to meet consumers' new needs. Thinking about SoLoMo helps us all in order to fine tune our marketing strategies. There are three simple questions that every marketing manager should ask while evaluating a marketing plan: Does it bring together the social, local, and mobile strengths of our product/service? Do we fully understand the SoLoMo needs of our consumers? Are we SoLoMo-ready? We are all SoLoMo after all!

References

Adobe, "Mobile Consumer Survey Results—Reaching and Building Loyalty With Your Most Valuable Mobile Customers." Retrieved April 24, 2015, from https://solutionpartners.adobe.com/content/dam/collateral/APEXAssets_Publ ic/54458_amc_mobile_survey_report_ue_v3.pdf, 2014.

Ankeny, J., "SoLoMo and How It Can Help Your Marketing." Retrieved June 5, 2015, from http://www.entrepreneur.com/article/226408, 2013

Armstrong, C.G., E.B. Delia, and M.D. Giardina, "Embracing the Social in Social Media. An Analysis of the Social Media Marketing Strategies of the Los Angeles Kings." *Communication & Sport*, 2167479514532914, 2014.

Balakrishnan, B.K.P.D., M.I. Dahnil, and W.J. Yi, "The Impact of Social Media Marketing Medium Toward Purchase Intention and Brand Loyalty Among Generation Y." Procedia-Social and Behavioral Sciences 148, 177–185, 2014.

Levesque, N., H. Boeck, F. Durif, and A. Bilolo., "The Impact of Proximity Marketing on Consumer Reactions and Firm Performance: A Conceptual and Integrative Model." In *Twenty-First Americas Conference on Information Systems*, Puerto Rico, 2015.

Bolen, A., "Seven Characteristics of the Modern Consumer." SAS Website. Retrieved May 5, 2014, from http://www.sas.com/en_us/insights/articles/marketing/modern-consumer.html, 2015.

Boyd, D.M., and N.B. Ellison, "Social Network Sites: Definition, History, and Scholarship." *Journal of Computer-Mediated Communication* 13, 210–230, 2008.

Bruno, T., *Wearable Technology: Smart Watches to Google Glass for Libraries.* Vol. 1. Lanham, MD: Rowman & Littlefield, 2015.

Brustein, J., "We Now Spend More Time Staring at Phones Than TVs." Retrieved April 2015, from http://www.bloomberg.com/bw/articles/2014-11-19/we-now-spend-more-time-staring-at-phones-than-tvs, 2014.

Buhalis, D., and E. Mamalakis, "Social Media Return on Investment and Performance Evaluation in the Hotel Industry Context." In Tussyadiah, I., and A. Iversini (eds.), *Information and Communication Technologies in Tourism 2015* (pp. 241–253). Cham: Springer International Publishing, 2015.

Chaffey, D. and F. Ellis-Chadwick, *Digital Marketing: Strategy, Implementation and Practice.* Englewood Cliffs, NJ: Prentice Hall, 2012.

Chan, J.M., and R. Yazdanifard, "How Social Media Marketing can Influence the Profitability of an Online Company From a Consumer Point of View." *Journal of Research in Marketing* 2, no. 2, 157–160, 2014.

Chaney, P., "Marketing to the 'SoLoMo' Consumer." Retrieved July 20, 2015, from http://webmarketingtoday.com/articles/Marketing-to-the-SoLoMo-Consumer/, 2015.

CISCO, "Gen Y: New Dawn for Work, Play, Identity." Retrieved from http://www.cisco.com/en/US/solutions/ns341/ns525/ns537/ns705/ns1120/2012-CCWTR-Chapter1-Global-Results.pdf, 2012.

comScore, "The impact of Connected Devices on Consumer Behavior—A Comparison of US and European Mobile Consumer Behavior." Retrieved February 11, 2015, from http://www.comscore.com/Insights/Presentations-and-Whitepapers/2013/The-Impact-of-Connected-Devices-on-Consumer-Behavior, 2013.

Cristo, D., "Does My Business Really Need a Mobile App?" Retrieved March 30, 2015, from http://marketingland.com/really-need-app-119528, 2015.

Deloitte, "Social Media and the Digital Enterprise." Retrieved November 21, 2015 from http://www2.deloitte.com/content/dam/Deloitte/us/Documents/risk/us-aers-social-media-digital-enterprise-100314.pdf, 2014.

Doyle, K., "SoLoMo—Why It Matters and What You Should Know." Retrieved April 10, 2015, from http://newsroom.cisco.com/feature-content?articleId=985956, 2012.

Dutot, V., "Factors Influencing Near Field Communication (NFC) Adoption: An Extended TAM Approach." *The Journal of High Technology Management Research* 26, no. 1, 45–57, 2015.

Econsultancy, "Quarterly Digital Intelligence Briefing: Finding the Path to Mobile Maturity." May, 2014.

Ericson, "Ericsson Mobility Report." Retrieved May 14, 2015 from http://www.ericsson.com/mobility-report, 2015.

Ericson, L., L. Herring, and K. Ungerman, "Busting Mobile-Shopping Myths—What Do Mobile Shoppers Really Want? Less Than Many Retailers Think." McKinsey & Company. Retrieved April 25, 2015, from http://www.mckinsey.com/insights/consumer_and_retail/busting_mobile_shopping_myths, 2014.

Eugen, P., A.A. Rahman, and P.-P. Doina, "Fundamentals of Smart Geolocation Solutions for Business." *Ovidius University Annals, Economic Sciences Series* 14, no. 1, 513–518, 2014.

Evans, D., *Social Media Marketing: An Hour a Day*. Indianapolis, IN: Wiley, 2012.

Flurry Analytics, "Messaging Apps Shatter Living Room Walls (and Sunday Usage Records) During the Super Bowl." Retrieved July 15, 2015, from http://flurrymobile.tumblr.com/post/115195168820/messaging-apps-shatter-living-room-walls-and, 2015.

Hoffman, D., and M. Fodor, "Can You Measure the ROI of Your Social Media Marketing?" *Sloan Management Review* 52, no. 1, 2010.

IAB Australia, "Multi-Screen Research." Retrieved May 6, 2015, from https://www.iabaustralia.com.au/uploads/uploads/2013-10/1382050800_d 38ae3a74556ba4540e1e67d4339ce77.pdf, 2013.

IpsosMediaCT, "The Connected Consumer: Different Screen Behavior." Retrieved May 23, 2015 from https://www.ipsos-mori.com/Assets/Docs /Publications/MediaCT_TP_Connected_Consumer1.pdf, 2014.

Kamins, M.A., "The Impact of Word of Mouth and the Facilitative Effects of Social Media." In Stewart, D.W. (ed.) *The Handbook of Persuasion and Social Marketing [3 volumes]* (pp. 129–149). Santa Barbara, CA: ABC-CLIO, LLC, 2014.

Kemp. S., "Global Digital Statshot August 2015: We Are Social's Compendium of Global Digital Statistics." Retrieved September 10, 2015, from http://wearesocial.net/tag/statshot/, 2015.

Kinnunen, M., S.Q. Mian, H. Oinas-Kukkonen, J. Riekki, M. Jutila, M. Ervasti, P. Ahokangas, and E. Alasaarela, "Wearable and Mobile Sensors Connected to Social Media in Human Well-Being Applications." *Telematics and Informatics* 33, no. 1, 92–101, 2016.

Lecinski, J., "Winning the Zero Moment of Truth. Ret Google." Retrieved July 24, 2015, from http://ssl.gstatic.com/think/docs/2012-zmot-handbook_ research-studies.pdf, 2012.

McKinsey, "iConsumer: Digital Consumers Altering the Value Chain." Retrieved May 25, 2015, from http://www.mckinsey.com/client_service /high_tech/iconsumer, 2013.

Miller, R., and N. Lammas, "Social media and its implications for viral marketing." *Asia Pacific Public Relations Journal*, 11, no. 1, 1–9, 2010.

Millward Brown, "AdReaction—Marketing in a Multiscreen World." Retrieved from https://www.millwardbrown.com/AdReaction/2014/report/Millward-Brown_AdReaction-2014_Global.pdf, 2014.

Mobile Marketing Association, "The Mobile Marketing Roadmap—How Mobile is Transforming Marketing for Targeting Next Generation Consumer." Mobile Marketing Association, 2013.

Motameni, R., and R. Nordstrom, "Correlating the Social Media Functionalities to Marketing Goals and Strategies." *Journal of Marketing Management* 2, 3–4, 2014.

Murugesan, S., "Understanding Web 2.0." *IT Pro,* July-August, 34–41, 2007.

Nielsen Research, "The Mobile Consumer: A Global Snapshot." Retrieved May 6, 2015, from http://www.nielsen.com/content/dam/corporate/us/en/reports-downloads/2013%20Reports/Mobile-Consumer-Report-2013.pdf, 2013.

Nielsen Research, "The Digital Consumer". Retrieved November 21, 2015 from http://www.nielsen.com/content/dam/corporate/us/en/reports-downloads /2014%20Reports/the-digital-consumer-report-feb-2014.pdf, 2014.

Oh, J.-S., C.-U. Park, and S.-B. Lee, "NFC-Based Mobile Payment Service Adoption and Diffusion." *Journal of Convergence* 5, no. 2, 2014.

Park, Y.J., and M. Skoric, "Personalized Ad in Your Google Glass? Wearable Technology, Hands-Off Data Collection, and New Policy Imperative." *Journal of Business Ethics*, 1–12, 2015.

Pew Research, "Social Media Usage: 2005–2015." Retrieved March 20, 2015, from http://www.pewinternet.org/2015/10/08/social-networking-usage-2005-2015/, 2015.

Pham, T. T., & Ho, J. C. The effects of product-related, personal-related factors and attractiveness of alternatives on consumer adoption of NFC-based mobile payments. *Technology In Society*, doi:10.1016/j.techsoc.2015.05 .004, 2015.

Prensky, M., "Digital Natives, Digital Immigrants." *On the Horizon*, 9, no. 5, 1–6, 2001.

Qualman, E., *Socialomics: How Social Media Transforms the Way We Live and Do Business*. Hoboken, NJ: Wiley & Sons, 2009.

Safko, L., and D.K. Brake, *The Social Media Bible: Tactics, Tools and Strategies for Business Success*. Hoboken, NJ: Wiley, 2009.

Santonocito, P., "Online Social Networking: What It Really Means to Employee Recruitment." *Online Recruitment Magazine*. Retrieved from http://www. onrec.com/sites/default/files/magazines/pdfs/Mag_Online.pdf, 2009.

Shiffman, D., *The Age of Engage: Reinventing Marketing for Today's Connected, Collaborative, and Hyper Interactive Culture*. Ladera Ranch, CA: Hunt Street Press, 2008.

Sterling, G., "Report: Mobile Users Spend 80 Percent of Time in Just Five Apps." Retrieved February 20, 2015, from http://marketingland.com /report-mobile-users-spend-80-percent-time-just-five-apps-116858, 2015.

The Economist, "Something New Under the Sun—A Special Report on Innovation." *The Economist*, October 13 2007.

Trendwatching, "Trendwatching Report." Retrieved April 9, 2015, from http://trendwatching.com/trends/brand-sacrifice/, 2014.

Tuten, T., and M.R. Solomon, "Social Media Marketing." London: SAGE Publications, 2014.

Weaver, A.C., and B.B. Morrison, "Social Networking." *Computer*, 41, 2, 2008.

Yamamoto, G.T., *Mobilized Marketing and the Consumer: Technological Developments and Challenges*. Hershey, PA: Business Science Reference, 2010.

Index